D0648927

HELLO WEB APP

Intermediate Concepts

by Tracy Osborn

Hello Web App: Intermediate Concepts
http://hellowebapp.com

ISBN 978-0-9863659-2-8

San Jose, California
http://limedaring.com

First Edition (1.0)
Printed in PRC

To the entire Django and Python community, since they've been nothing but welcoming and encouraging and I am truly grateful to work in such a wonderful industry.

And to my husband Andrey who is unfailingly my biggest supporter and cheerleader. Without him, I wouldn't be where I am today.

(Quick high-five to my cat and dog.)

TABLE OF CONTENTS

INTRODUCTION

Welcome to *Hello Web App*, the sequel!

A year ago, I wrote *Hello Web App*, a book that walks new programmers through building their own web app. It won't help you get a degree in Computer Science or Computer Engineering, nor is it a guide to getting a job as a developer or an engineer. Simply, the book helps people learn how to build web apps.

Readers can decide what's next after *Hello Web App*: learn more to become an engineer, hack on web apps as side-projects, or start building a lifestyle business or a startup (I did the last option and it turned out pretty awesome). *Hello Web App* is the next step in the learn-to-code revolution—we can go beyond learning how to just build a static website with HTML and CSS, we can build a fully functional web app and start working with customers.

All of this started after I taught myself—painfully—how to code half a decade ago (holy moly does time fly). I was a designer with an Art degree and loved doing front-end web development work. I had a lot of ideas for websites I wanted to build, but didn't want to hire someone to do the back-end development work for me.

After a few months of learning, I was able to cobble together a basic web app from several Django tutorials on the web with copious amounts of help from my friends, and eventually launched a website. This website grew into my startup (and I the solo founder at the helm), which was accepted into a prominent startup accelerator and eventually raised funding.

During the years of refining my startup, I've learned more and more about web app development. The only tutorials available were frustratingly aimed at other developers—people who already knew how to code and who understood the jargon, references and side-notes. As I learned more development, I began to have mini-epiphanies: "Why the heck was it taught *that* way when it could be taught *this* way?" I realized that we needed a better way to teach web app development to those who didn't already know how to code. After years of waiting for this to be built and seeing no progress, I decided to write the book myself.

Hello Web App was Kickstarted in 2014 and launched on May 4th, 2015. Since then, thousands of folks have used the *Hello Web App* tutorial to create their first web app. The goal was to write a short, easy introduction to web app development, meaning the original book is the size of a small paperback. *Hello Web App* takes you from creating a project idea to launching your app on the internet so you can start working with real customers.

Consider this book, *Hello Web App: Intermediate Concepts*, as the whipped cream on top of a basic web app sundae. The chapters here don't rely on a chronological order, so you don't need to go directly from chapter to the next through the end of the book. Here, you can pick the chapter and concept you want to learn and just start building.

Also keep in mind that you don't need to have read the original *Hello Web App* for this book to be of use to you. Got a basic Django web app and want to take it to the next level? This book is for you.

This book is not going to have a lot of Computer-Science-y acronyms and engineering concepts. There are a lot of tutorials out there that will teach you Computer Science theory and best practices. Here, you'll learn how to do something from start to finish without a lot of asides and explanation about the why—just the how. And a *tiny* bit of theory.

We're building web apps, so we can create cool side projects—maybe even starting a lifestyle business or becoming the next startup. Learning web app development will open up so many doors for you.

Prerequisites

As mentioned before, this is a follow-up to the original *Hello Web App* but experience with the original book is **not required**. Do you have a basic Django web app and want to build some of the topics this book covers, like payment functionality? I got you.

One side-note: This book references the command-line command touch to create new files. Mac and Linux computers have this ability natively, but unfortunately Windows computers don't. Either create the new files in your code-editor of choice by hand, or you can use Git for Windows (http:// hellowebapp.com/ic/1), which installs Git on your computer in addition to giving you a command line interface that lets you do UNIX commands such as touch.

Our discussion forum

If you have any issues while going through this book and Googling your question isn't giving you the answers you seek, check out the awesome *Hello Web App* discussion forum here: http://discuss.hellowebapp.com

Feel free to create a new topic if you're stuck and I'll pop in to help you within a few days (or some of the other awesome commentators may get back to you sooner). I also encourage you to share the app you've made for feedback, ask questions, or just say hi.

All right, let's get started!

1 | CHAPTER 1
CREATING A CONTACT FORM AND WORKING WITH CUSTOM FORMS

IN THIS WALKTHROUGH, WE'RE GOING TO BUILD SOMETHING relatively easy: a simple contact form where your users can enter their name, email address, and message, which will be emailed to you automatically by your website (with the user's email as the reply-to). In terms of the big picture, this will teach you how to create custom forms using Django, as so far in Hello Web App, we've only shown you how to create a `ModelForm`.

Set up the URL

Pretty much every new feature that will go into your web app will go through the same process: set up the URL, set up the logic, then set up the template. We're going to set up a simple page that lives at *contact/*. Add the new page to your *urls.py*:

urls.py
```
# make sure you're importing your views
from collection import views
```

```
urlpatterns = [
    ...
    # new url definition
    url(r'^contact/$', views.contact, name='contact'),
```

Set up the view

Now in *views.py*, we need to start setting up the logic. Let's set it up to just display a form for now. Later on, we'll do the rest of the logic for after the form is submitted in a bit:

views.py
```
# add to the top
from collection.forms import ContactForm

# add to your views
def contact(request):
    form_class = ContactForm

    return render(request, 'contact.html', {
        'form': form_class,
    })
```

We're grabbing a form (which we haven't defined yet) and passing it over into the template (which we haven't created yet).

Set up the form

In *Hello Web App*, we went over creating forms with Model-Forms, but skipped creating basic forms without a model. But it's just as simple to create custom forms!

In our *forms.py*, add the below form code:

```
```

forms.py

```python
# make sure this is at the top if it isn't already
from django import forms
# our new form
class ContactForm(forms.Form):
    contact_name = forms.CharField()
    contact_email = forms.EmailField()
    content = forms.CharField(widget=forms.Textarea)
```

We're going to define the fields we want in our form, which will be just the contact's name, their email, and what they'd like to say to you.

All those form fields were grabbed from Django's form fields documentation (http://hellowebapp.com/ic/2), which is pretty easy to read to see what other fields are available. We're making all the form fields required, using an EmailField for the email so we can take advantage of the additional email formatting checks that Django provides, and making the "content" field a Textarea.

Create the template

Now we need to create the template to display the contact form on our website. We're going to create the form using the form passed in from our view.

contact.html

```html
{% extends 'base.html' %}
{% block title %}Contact - {{ block.super }}{% endblock %}
{% block content %}
<h1>Contact</h1>
<form role="form" action="" method="post">
    {% csrf_token %}
    {{ form.as_p }}
    <button type="submit">Submit</button>
</form>
{% endblock %}
```

At this point, we have all the pieces in place to display the form. Load */contact/* and check it out:

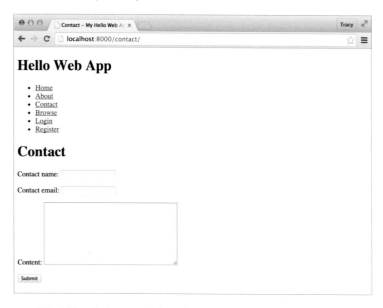

Nice! Now let's start adding the logic in the back-end to handle the information submitted by the user.

Set up your local email server

This will be redundant for you if you've already finished already the *Hello Web App* tutorial. In case you haven't, all you need to do to set up a local email server is add these lines to the bottom of your *settings.py*:

settings.py

```
EMAIL_BACKEND = 'django.core.mail.backends.console.EmailBackend'
DEFAULT_FROM_EMAIL = 'testing@example.com'
EMAIL_HOST_USER = ''
EMAIL_HOST_PASSWORD = ''
EMAIL_USE_TLS = False
EMAIL_PORT = 1025
```

This tells Django to output the "email" to your console, where you ran your `python manage.py runserver` command. We'll see what this looks like in a second.

(This is only for local development—we'll get into email servers for your production web app at the end of this chapter.)

Add the email logic

Let's fill out the rest of the email logic. Here's the view from before, now filled in:

views.py

```
# new imports that go at the top of the file
from django.template.loader import get_template
from django.core.mail import EmailMessage
from django.template import Context

# our view
def contact(request):
    form_class = ContactForm

    # new logic!
    if request.method == 'POST':
        form = form_class(data=request.POST)

        if form.is_valid():
            contact_name = form.cleaned_data['contact_name']
            contact_email = form.cleaned_data['contact_email']
            form_content = form.cleaned_data['content']

            # email the profile with the contact info
            template = get_template('contact_template.txt')

            context = Context({
                'contact_name': contact_name,
                'contact_email': contact_email,
```

```
        'form_content': form_content,
    })
    content = template.render(context)

    email = EmailMessage(
        'New contact form submission',
        content,
        'Your website <hi@weddinglovely.com>',
        ['youremail@gmail.com'],
        headers = {'Reply-To': contact_email }
    )
    email.send()
    return redirect('contact')

return render(request, 'contact.html', {
    'form': form_class,
})
```

Phew, a lot of logic! If you read it from top to bottom, here's what's happening if the form was submitted:

- Apply the information from the form to the form class we set up before.

- Make sure that everything is valid (no missing fields, etc.)

- Take the form information and put it in variables.

- Stick the form information into a contact form template (which we will create momentarily).

- Create an email message using that contact template, and send the message.

- Redirect to our contact page (not ideal, we'll go into why below).

- Otherwise, just create the template with a blank form.

Create a template for your email

Before we can test our logic, we need to create an email template. Our email template is going to be simple, as it will just show the sections that our user filled out. Create a new file in your templates directory (touch contact_template.txt) and fill it in with the info below. Django will grab this file and fill it in using the context we set up in the view.

contact_template.txt
```
Contact Name: {{ contact_name|striptags }}
Email: {{ contact_email|striptags }}
Content: {{ form_content|striptags }}
```

(We're using Django's template filter strip_tags to strip out HTML from the content. We need to be very careful with taking user input and presenting it as it was given. If we don't strip HTML, then a malicious user might put in some evil JavaScript in their input!)

Improve the form (optional)

In the screenshot of the form from before, we can see that the labels of the form aren't very "pretty"—for example, just saying "Contact name," which is very impersonal.

Django creates these names automatically from your field names, but we can set up our own pretty label names in the form definition in *forms.py*. To do so, update your code to the below:

forms.py
```
class ContactForm(forms.Form):
    contact_name = forms.CharField(required=True)
    contact_email = forms.EmailField(required=True)
```

```
content = forms.CharField(
    required=True,
    widget=forms.Textarea
)

# the new bit we're adding
def __init__(self, *args, **kwargs):
    super(ContactForm, self).__init__(*args, **kwargs)
    self.fields['contact_name'].label = "Your name:"
    self.fields['contact_email'].label = "Your email:"
    self.fields['content'].label = "What do you want to say?"
```

We've added the bit that starts with __init__, which might look a bit confusing. If you ignore the first two lines, the rest are pretty easy to read. We're just grabbing the relevant fields in our form and updating the label.

We can set more than just the label—we can also set the field as required, add help text, and other fields as well through __init__. You can see more information about updating form fields and attributes here in this excellent post: http://hellowebapp.com/ic/3

Once we've reloaded our form, we can see the new labels:

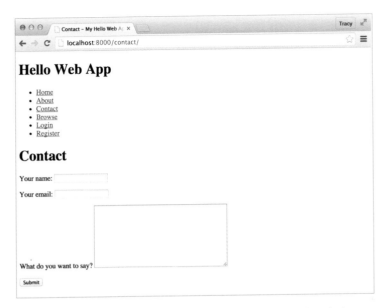

(Of course, this is minus any pretty CSS styling we need to do.)

Once we stick in some test information and submit the form, we can see the "email" in our command line:

```
Django version 1.8.4, using settings 'hellowebapp.settings'
Starting development server at http://127.0.0.1:8000/
Quit the server with CONTROL-C.
[03/Oct/2015 18:15:27] "GET /contact/ HTTP/1.1" 200 1412
[03/Oct/2015 18:15:27] "GET /static/css/style.css HTTP/1.1" 200 37
[03/Oct/2015 18:15:28] "GET /favicon.ico HTTP/1.1" 404 4250
MIME-Version: 1.0
Content-Type: text/plain; charset="utf-8"
Content-Transfer-Encoding: 7bit
Subject: New contact form submission
From: Your website<hi@weddinglovely.com>
To: youremail@gmail.com
Date: Sat, 03 Oct 2015 18:16:54 -0000
Message-ID: <20151003181654.87128.78963@Orion.local>
Reply-To: test@test.com

Contact Name: Test
Email: test@test.com
Content: Hi, this is a test message!

------------------------------------------------------------------
[03/Oct/2015 18:16:55] "POST /contact/ HTTP/1.1" 302 0
[03/Oct/2015 18:16:55] "GET /contact/ HTTP/1.1" 200 1412
```

Set up your live email server (optional)

The local email server will output "emails" to your local server (what's running in your command line), so you can confirm everything is working locally. But, when your web app is live, you obviously want those emails to actually land in your email inbox, rather than the server output.

You can do this by setting up something like Sendgrid (http://hellowebapp.com/ic/4) or Mandrill (http://hellowebapp.com/ic/5)—freemium email servers where you should just need to sign up for an account and set the details of your account in your *settings.py*.

Sendgrid has a great short walkthrough here: http://hellowebapp.com/ic/6. If you're at the point in *Hello Web App* where you've set up a production settings file, you can stick the email server stuff in there, and keep your local/test emails (using the Django console) in your normal *settings.py* file. This way you can "send emails" as you're developing your app, but you don't have to worry about going over the daily email limit that these email delivery products have in their freemium accounts.

Things that could be improved

I mentioned above that, upon successful form submission, you will be redirected to your app homepage. That would be really confusing to the user, because there is no success message. You have two options here:

- **Set up a separate template that just says "Success!" that users are redirected to after successful submission.** This is the easiest option, but adding these kind of templates tends to clutter up your templates directory.

- **Utilize the Django messages framework.** This is a better option. In your base template file, you can add a "messages" block, and then when you redirect to a page, you could pass along a message (e.g. an alert, an error, a warning, an info message, etc.) that will pop into the top of any page. It's what I use for my production web apps. Chapter 6, *Setting up Django Messages for Alerts*, goes into this in detail.

Your contact form is complete!

You now have a working contact form that allows visitors to your web app to email you messages, and hopefully you learned some new skills about creating forms in Django and working with email. Congrats!

2 | CHAPTER 2
ADDING A NEW MODEL

STORY TIME! BACK WHEN I STARTED MY FIRST APP (a directory of wedding invitation designers), I launched a very small, very minimal version with just enough features—basically everything that was built in the original *Hello Web App* tutorial—and added more features and functionality as the web app grew in traffic.

Over time, I added new fields that the designers could fill out for their profile (like their social media profiles, and new photo slots), and each of these new profile fields was added as a new line in my `Profile` model.

That one model listed everything for the profile, and at one point (full disclosure!), looked like this:

```
# pro profiles
is_pro_profile = models.BooleanField(default=False)
twitter_url = models.CharField(max_length=15, blank=True)
facebook_url = models.CharField(max_length=80, blank=True)
banner_image = ImageField(
    upload_to=get_profile_image_path('banner.jpg'),
    blank=True, null=True)
```

```python
avatar_image = ImageField(
    upload_to=get_profile_image_path('avatar.jpg'),
    blank=True, null=True)

# pro profiles extra images
portfolio_image_1 = ImageField(
    upload_to=get_profile_image_path('1.jpg'),
    blank=True, null=True)
portfolio_image_2 = ImageField(
    upload_to=get_profile_image_path('2.jpg'),
    blank=True, null=True)
portfolio_image_3 = ImageField(
    upload_to=get_profile_image_path('3.jpg'),
    blank=True, null=True)
portfolio_image_4 = ImageField(
    upload_to=get_profile_image_path('4.jpg'),
    blank=True, null=True)
portfolio_image_5 = ImageField(
    upload_to=get_profile_image_path('5.jpg'),
    blank=True, null=True)
portfolio_image_6 = ImageField(
    upload_to=get_profile_image_path('6.jpg'),
    blank=True, null=True)
portfolio_image_7 = ImageField(
    upload_to=get_profile_image_path('7.jpg'),
    blank=True, null=True)
portfolio_image_8 = ImageField(
    upload_to=get_profile_image_path('8.jpg'),
    blank=True, null=True)
portfolio_image_9 = ImageField(
    upload_to=get_profile_image_path('9.jpg'),
    blank=True, null=True)
```

This is actual embarrassing code from my app in 2012. It worked, yes. But it wasn't a good idea, and I didn't learn why for a long time. Do you know why the above isn't the greatest idea?

In this chapter, I'm going to teach you what **not** to do and why so that when building your models and databases you don't have problems like the above in your model.

Proper schema design: multiple tables can be better than just one big table

Eventually, I moved from one giant model holding everything to three different models: one holding only profile information, one holding social media information, and one holding images.

There are a couple different reasons why having one big table is not the best idea:

- If a new, awesome social network started, I'd have to add another line to my model, adding a new row to the database.

- Same thing with images—I simply can't have a *dynamic* number of images. If I have fifteen slots allocated for images, then those 15 slots will exist for every object in my database. If some objects use just one image or 15 images, they'll both be stored the same way—15 image columns per row. If I wanted to support 16 images, I'd need to run a migration again to change the schema. On the other hand, if I used a separate table to store images (where each row is one image associated with a profile), then my objects can have as many (or as few) images as needed without updating the schema and running migrations.

Plus, there are quite a few other reasons to parcel out your user data into multiple models:

- Some queries become a lot easier to perform, such as "how many images am I storing?" If you have one giant model, you'd need to go through every row and check how many of the 15 image columns have an image in them and then sum those up. By using a separate table, you just have to check how many rows are in that table and then you're done.

- Think of a hypothetical meme-sharing site. We could have a model for our images, a model for our contributors' profiles, and a model to hold captions for the images contributed by our users. The model with captions can act as a bridge between the profile model and image models, as well as storing extra information like the caption.

- Let's say we wanted to track votes for the best memes. We'd have a profile table, the meme table, and in between them we would have a vote table which is an association from the profile to the meme. This lets us query things like "What are Tracy's favorite memes?" or "Which meme has the most votes?" all while restricting people to only vote once per meme—something we couldn't do if we only stored a vote count on the meme and incremented it each time.

Let's fix the social media example mentioned above by making a new model to hold our social media accounts.

How to add a new model to your app

We've been all talk and no coding so far in this chapter! Time to fix that.

I'm going to go through a very simple demonstration of how to add a new model to your app that will hold social media information, essentially solving the first problem I had in the example above from my old app.(We'll solve the images problem in Chapter 4, *Adding User-Uploaded Images.*)

Open up your *models.py* and add the new model:

models.py

```
class Social(models.Model):
    SOCIAL_TYPES = (
        ('twitter', 'Twitter'),
        ('facebook', 'Facebook'),
        ('pinterest', 'Pinterest'),
        ('instagram', 'Instagram'),
    )
    network = models.CharField(max_length=255,
        choices=SOCIAL_TYPES)
    username = models.CharField(max_length=255)
    thing = models.ForeignKey(Thing,
        related_name="social_accounts")
```

We're going to have columns for the network name as well as the username on those accounts, and basically give an "owner" of this extra model—tying it to a parent Thing.

We're also going to do something a bit new here, and define a list of social media choices rather than allowing free form input. SOCIAL_TYPES is a "tuple" of tuples (a *tuple* is like a special list that can't be changed by the app while it's running) using Python with our social media choices (I'm not listing all, feel free to add more). Then we're telling the model that the acceptable choices for this field are in that list. The first element in the tuple is the actual value used in the model, and the second element is the human-readable version.

Since we updated our *models.py*, we need to run a migration:

```
$ python manage.py makemigrations
Migrations for 'collection':
  0006_social.py:
    - Create model Social
```

If it was successful, then you can migrate the app:

```
Operations to perform:
  Synchronize unmigrated apps: registration
```

```
  Apply all migrations: admin, contenttypes, collection, auth, sessions
Synchronizing apps without migrations:
  Creating tables...
  Installing custom SQL...
  Installing indexes...
Running migrations:
  Applying collection.0006_social... OK
```

Add to your admin

Since you've added a new model, now you need to add it to
your Django admin in *admin.py* like usual:

admin.py
```
# make sure to import Social at the top
from collection.models import Thing, Social

# our new admin for the Social model
class SocialAdmin(admin.ModelAdmin):
    model = Social
    list_display = ('network', 'username',)

# don't forget to register at the end
admin.site.register(Social, SocialAdmin)
```

Cool, now you can see your new model in the admin:

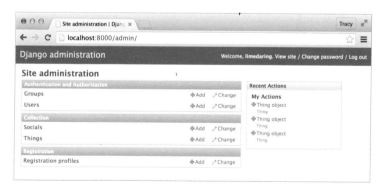

I'm not a fan of Django using the name "Socials" (it automatically takes your model name, capitalizes it and pluralizes it for the admin view.) It's easy to change it, though. Just add a Meta class to your model:

models.py
```
class Social(models.Model):
    SOCIAL_TYPES = (
        ('twitter', 'Twitter'),
        ('facebook', 'Facebook'),
        ('pinterest', 'Pinterest'),
        ('instagram', 'Instagram'),
    )

    network = models.CharField(max_length=255,
        choices=SOCIAL_TYPES)
    username = models.CharField(max_length=255)
    thing = models.ForeignKey(Thing,
        related_name="social_accounts")

    # where we're overriding the admin name
    class Meta:
        verbose_name_plural = "Social media links"
```

A list of all the Meta options you can add to your model can be found here: http://hellowebapp.com/ic/7

Refresh, and voilà, the admin is updated:

Fun trick!

Add a couple fake social media accounts tied to an object in your main model. You can see that the choices are working:

Next, let's see how we can show these social links on our Thing pages.

Access the new view from your views

Let's update the individual object page on your app to list out the social media profiles it has.

views.py

```python
def thing_detail(request, slug):
    # grab the object...
    thing = Thing.objects.get(slug=slug)

    # new line! grab all the object's social accounts
    social_accounts = thing.social_accounts.all()

    # and pass to the template
    return render(request, 'things/thing_detail.html', {
        'thing': thing,
        'social_accounts': social_accounts,
    })
```

We've added one new line in which we're grabbing all the social media accounts that are tied to that object. Then, of course, accessing it from the template is easy. You just need to add a loop somewhere in your template:

thing_detail.html

```html
{% if social_accounts %}
<ul>
    {% for social_account in social_accounts %}
    <li>
        <a href="http://{{ social_account.network }}
            .com/{{ social_account.username }}">
            {{ social_account.network|title }}
        </a>
    </li>
    {% endfor %}
</ul>
{% endif %}
```

If the list of objects that you're passing has social media accounts, then you can create an HTML list, and then list out the networks, linking to the account. Since the networks we set in the choices before are also the URLs for those networks anyways, it allows us to smartly set the URL for the link to go to.

We'll talk more about databases in Chapter 13, *Database Pitfalls*, since there are more important schema design and database design stuff that we've glossed over. But essentially, now you know how and why for creating new models in your app!

CHAPTER 3

ADDING EASY ADMIN EMAILS, HELPERS, SITEMAPS, AND MORE

THIS CHAPTER WILL COVER A LOT OF SHORT, FUN THINGS that wouldn't fill out a full chapter that you can add to your web app! We're going to quickly go over an admin email shortcut, abstract models, model helper functions, and sitemaps.

Adding an admin email shortcut to your views

On some occasions, I want my app to send me an email. For example, when a user upgrades their account, I want to be alerted immediately rather than having to continuously check my admin dashboard. We've covered how to set up emails in the original *Hello Web App* tutorial, and there is a much quicker shortcut method we can use when sending emails to our app admins.

Add these settings to your *settings.py*:

settings.py

```python
# the email address that the "server emails" will come from
SERVER_EMAIL = 'app_email@mydomain.com'

# the email you want these admin emails to go to
# (can add as many as you like)
ADMINS = [
    ('your name', 'me@mydomain.com'),
]
```

If you add more emails to the admins list, don't forget to add the trailing commas.

Then, in our code, this is all we need to do in our views to send an email to the admins listed in our settings:

```python
# you'll need to import this
from django.core.mail import mail_admins

# add this anywhere in your views to send a message
mail_admins("Our subject line", "Our content")
```

I use this shortcut all over my views to alert me immediately if anything happens that shouldn't happen, or if I need immediate notifications of something good (like a user signing up). Handy function!

Adding created and last-modified dates using an abstract model

In the original *Hello Web App* tutorial, I showed you how to create a basic model, but missed something super useful—created and modified dates. With these, you can easily sort your database objects by last added, first added, what profiles were most recently updated (or not updated in a long time) and more time-based filtering needs.

We're going to create an *abstract* model, which we can then tie to our main model. Sound confusing? Should be easy enough to understand by looking at the code:

models.py

```python
class Timestamp(models.Model):
    created = models.DateTimeField(auto_now_add=True)
    updated = models.DateTimeField(auto_now=True)

    class Meta:
        abstract = True

# don't forget to update your model's inheritance
class Thing(Timestamp):
    name = models.CharField(max_length=255)
    # the rest of our model fields...
```

We've added a new model called Timestamp with two fields—created, with a DateTimeField with auto_now_add=True (which means Django will update this field automatically with the date and time when it's created); and updated, with a DateTimeField with auto_now=True (which means Django will automatically update this field whenever the model updates). We've also added a Meta class, setting abstract=True—meaning, this isn't a real model, don't create a table for it.

Finally, we updated our main model from inheriting directly from Django's models.Model to inheriting from Timestamp. It's like we inserted Timestamp in the middle of our model and Django, adding the extra Timestamp fields on top of our existing fields. If we add other models which also need those timestamps, we can just inherit from Timestamp rather than models.Model for those as well. This means we're repeating less code, which is always a good thing in programmer-land.

Now, if you're adding these fields to an existing model and make a migration (remember, `python manage.py makemigrations`) as you should, you'll get a fun error:

```
$ python manage.py makemigrations
You are trying to add a non-nullable field 'added' to thing
without a default; we can't do that (the database needs some-
thing to populate existing rows).
Please select a fix:
   1) Provide a one-off default now (will be set on all existing rows)
   2) Quit, and let me add a default in models.py
Select an option:
```

Django says, "Hey, this field is required, but it will be empty if I add it and that's not allowed. What should I do?"

Type 1 (we'll provide a one-off default) and enter:

```
Select an option: 1
Please enter the default value now, as valid Python
The datetime and django.utils.timezone modules are available,
so you can do e.g. timezone.now()
```

We're going to use exactly what Django recommends—`time-zone.now()`, to fill in those fields. Now, that will mean our created dates won't actually be correct for our existing data (because the created date will be set to the current date and time, rather than when that object was actually created) but it will be correct for all data going forward. Type in `timezone.now()`, run through the same process with the other field (as it will have the same problem) and the migration file should be created.

```
Please select a fix:
   1) Provide a one-off default now (will be set on all existing rows)
   2) Quit, and let me add a default in models.py
Select an option: 1
```

```
Please enter the default value now, as valid Python
The datetime and django.utils.timezone modules are available,
so you can do e.g.
timezone.now()
>>> timezone.now()
Migrations for 'collection':
  0004_auto_20150825_0145.py:
    - Add field added to thing
    - Add field updated to thing
```

Yay, now our objects have created and modified dates attached
to them! Not only that, you now know basically how to fill in
existing rows in your database when you make your migration
file.

One last thing—these dates will not show up in the admin, so
you can't update them yourself manually. The modified date
will change whenever data is saved (whether in your app or in
the admin) and the created date will always stay the same, so
the data will always be accurate.

Don't forget to run `python manage.py migrate` after the
migration file is created.

Helper functions on your model

When we're querying for data from our model, we know we
can use the syntax `modelname.modelfield` to grab the field
from the model—for example, `thing.name`. We can also set up
our own fields that will run some logic and return extra information as well, saving us some calculations and extra code in
our views.

We're going to add a few example helper methods to our
main model:

models.py

```
class Thing(models.Model):
    name = models.CharField(max_length=255)
    description = models.TextField()
    slug = models.SlugField()
    user = models.OneToOneField(User, blank=True, null=True)

    # new helper method
    def get_absolute_url(self):
        return "/things/%s/" % self.slug
```

This isn't something provided by Django—we're writing it
from scratch. The individual pages for these things are under
the URL */things/THING-SLUG/*, and if we ever needed to link
to the Thing's individual page (without using Django's fancy
URL helper), instead of putting `<a href="/things/{{ thing.
slug }}/"`, we could instead have `<a href="{{ thing.get_
absolute_url }}">`.

(Also, "`get_absolute_url`" is a part of Django's API. If you use
this exact method name, the Django admin will refer to it to
find the URL of an object, and it can use this to create "view
on site" links to take you from an object in the admin system
to the object's view on the site. So, by using this conventional
name, you'll also get this benefit. More information: http://
hellowebapp.com/ic/8)

There are all sorts of helpers you can write to return data from
your model in a different fashion. For example, in my startup, I
have a lot of helpers like this:

```
class Profile(models.Model):
    ...
    def has_specialized_directory(self):
        if self.directory in options.SPECIALIZED_DIR_VENDORS_LIST:
            return True
        return False
```

If this object's directory type is in a list, I return `True`; otherwise return `False`. That means in my templates and in my views, I can test `if object.has_specialized_directory` and do something special depending on the case. Very handy way to move some of your logic and computations into the model and create helpers.

Adding sitemaps

A sitemap is a file that lists out every page that is in your website—usually used to submit to Google so Google can easily crawl every page and add it to the Google search results. (This can happen on its own but it's faster if we first tell Google what pages exist.)

Django makes it pretty easy to add a sitemap file to your website. First, we need to add `'django.contrib.sitemaps'` to our INSTALLED_APPS:

settings.py
```
INSTALLED_APPS = (
    ...
    'django.contrib.sitemaps',
    ...
)
```

Then we need to create a file to hold our sitemap code in our app (the directory with *models.py*, which is named *collection* if you're using the original *Hello Web App* tutorial):

```
$ cd collection
collection $ touch sitemap.py
```

Inside our *sitemap.py*, we're going to create sitemap classes which will basically group our content. Think of your web app as sections. For the *Hello Web App* original tutorial, we have our individual object pages (which can be one section) and our miscellaneous one-off pages (e.g. homepage, browse page, about, content, etc.) as another section.

Here's how the sitemap code will look for those two sections:

sitemap.py

```python
import datetime
from django.contrib.sitemaps import Sitemap
from django.core.urlresolvers import reverse
from collection.models import Thing

class ThingSitemap(Sitemap):
    changefreq = "weekly"
    priority = 0.5

    def items(self):
        return Thing.objects.all()

    def lastmod(self, obj):
        return obj.updated

class StaticSitemap(Sitemap):
    lastmod = None
    priority = 0.5
    changefreq = "weekly"

    def items(self):
        return ['about', 'contact', 'browse',]

    def location(self, item):
        return reverse(item)

class HomepageSitemap(Sitemap):
    priority = 1
    changefreq = "daily"
```

```
def items(self):
    return ['home',]

def lastmod(self, obj):
    return datetime.date.today()

def location(self, item):
    return reverse(item)
```

Boom, that's a lot. We'll get into the explanation in a second, but right now let's just get it up in our browser so you can see it working.

Next, we need to add the URL to our *urls.py*:

urls.py
```
# add at the top
from django.contrib.sitemaps.views import sitemap
from collection.sitemap import (
    ThingSitemap,
    StaticSitemap,
    HomepageSitemap,
)
sitemaps = {
    'things': ThingSitemap,
    'static': StaticSitemap,
    'homepage': HomepageSitemap,
}

# then add below in your urlpatterns
urlpatterns = [
    ...
    url(r'^sitemap.xml$', sitemap, {'sitemaps': sitemaps},
        name='django.contrib.sitemaps.views.sitemap'),
```

This looks a little different than our normal URLs. We're passing in a dictionary with the sitemap classes we wrote into Django's sitemap code, which will build sitemaps from the items in the dictionary.

Head over to *http://localhost:8000/sitemap.xml* and check it out!

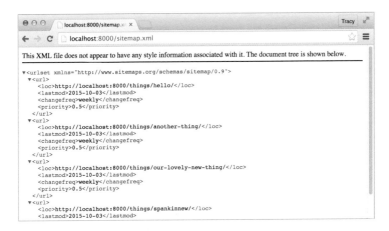

Welcome to the sitemap for your website! You can see that each page in your website (if added to *sitemap.py*) is listed along with these pieces of information:

- `<loc>`: The URL of the page.

- `<lastmod>`: The last time the page was modified (so search engines know how old the information is).

- `<changefreq>`: How often this page changes, which tells search engines approximately how often to come back and check for new information.

- `<priority>`: The importance of the page on your website, "1" being top priority.

(Note: Priority is just our recommendation to Google and other search engines; it isn't guaranteed that they'll listen to us!)

Now that we know this, we can take a look at our *sitemap.py* and the sections start making sense. You can see each sitemap class allows you to update the `changefreq`, `lastmod`, and `priority`—either setting a value for everything in that sitemap section, or using data from the database (see `def lastmod` on the `ThingSitemap`).

In each sitemap, we can also define the items included. Take a look at `StaticSitemap` and `HomepageSitemap`: we use `def items` to list out the pages we want to include (using the page's URL name), and then use `def location` with Django's `reverse` method which will magically figure out the correct URL for that page.

In `ThingSitemap`, we're grabbing our objects in the database. We don't have to set `def location` because we added `get_absolute_url` to the model in the last section, so Django already knows how to grab that information (through more magic). As for defining our items, we can use a `QuerySet`. You don't have to use `.all()`—you can change that to `.filter()` and grab only objects you want shown. For example, if you have "active" and "inactive" objects (set with a Boolean flag on your model), you'd probably only want to include active objects in your sitemap.

You might be wondering why the homepage has its own sitemap. It's just so we can set that one page with a priority of "1," since it's the most important page. Again, Google and other search engines don't necessary follow this information but it's still good practice. Also, setting all sitemaps to max priority doesn't do much as priorities are relative to one another (so all max priorities actually means they're all equally important, rather than some pages being more important than others).

Yay, sitemaps! If you don't have a Google Webmaster Tools account yet, head over here and create one: http://hellowe-bapp.com/ic/9. Then you can submit your new sitemap directly to Google so it can crawl it faster.

For more information about sitemaps, check out these pages:

- Sitemaps.org, for general information about sitemaps in general: http://hellowebapp.com/ic/10

- Django's sitemap documentation: http://hellowebapp.com/ic/11

A bit about class-based views and Django's generic views

So far in Hello Web App, I've only taught what's known as "function-based views"—our views are basically a top-down run-through of everything that's happening, and generally, there is one view per URL.

There is another style that is popular with Django and Django-nauts called "class-based views." This concept is a little harder to grok because it deals with Python classes and treating Django views as a class rather than a function. This means that class-based views fit better with object-oriented programming, and it also explains why class-based views are so popular with experienced programmers who already have an extensive background coding in object-oriented languages. If you've heard of class inheritance and mixins, this is where these concepts can be beneficial. If you want to write your own class-based views, check out this resource for more information: http://hellowebapp.com/ic/12).

Better, we can use the class-based views that Django provides us. Django comes with what's known as "generic class-based views" (or GCBVs) which are a kind of pre-made helpers that we can use wholesale or build our own class-based views on top of them.

We've already used generic class-based views in the original *Hello Web App*, but I just didn't bring attention to it.

```python
from django.views.generic import TemplateView, RedirectView

urlpatterns = [
    ...
    url(r'^about/$',
        TemplateView.as_view(template_name='about.html'),
        name='about'),
    url(r'^things/$',
        RedirectView.as_view(pattern_name='browse')),
```

These URLs allow us to skip writing our own views. For */about/*, we're using TemplateView to show a static template. For */things/*, we're using RedirectView to redirect to */browse/*.

More typically, Django's generic class-based views are subclassed in your own views, this will allow us to specify a small piece of behavior. For example:

```python
from django.views.generic.list import ListView
from collection.models import Thing

class ThingListView(ListView):
    model = Thing
```

In this example, we're using ListView—a generic class-based view that takes care of generating a page with a list of all the objects of some model. ListView looks at the model property to determine which model to list, so all we need to do is override it and ListView takes care of the rest. We can refer to the

documentation to see what else we can override:
http://hellowebapp.com/ic/13

In a nutshell, these generic class-based views give us shortcuts for our own code. The downside is that they might not feel as transparent as function-based views since functionality might be stowed away in layers of subclasses. When used appropriately, class-based views can make re-using pieces of functionality really easy and convenient. You'll notice that they're often the preferred approach of advanced developers.

This is a very short introduction that glosses over a lot of concepts with class-based views. For more info, check out these resources:

- Django's Introduction to Class-Based Views:
  http://hellowebapp.com/ic/14

- Classy Class-Based Views, which lists out all attributes and methods of Django's generic class-based views:
  http://hellowebapp.com/ic/15

- GoDjango's video on class-based views:
  http://hellowebapp.com/ic/16

- Last but not least, Kenneth Love wrote this great blog post on class-based views for *Hello Web App* readers:
  http://hellowebapp.com/ic/17

4 | CHAPTER 4
ADDING USER-UPLOADED IMAGES

MOST APPS WILL WANT TO LET THEIR USERS UPLOAD IMAGES. For my original web app, an invitation designer directory, my users needed to upload images to their profile page to showcase their design work. Unfortunately, adding user-uploaded images to your app isn't the simplest of tasks.

This chapter will walk you through adding an image field to your model, setting up the form on your templates to upload an image, and adding a way to delete images from your templates. Your users will be able to add images to their account and showcase them on their page on your website.

Adding a model for images

We're going to create a separate model to hold images. We could just stick an `ImageField` on our main model (which was named `Thing` in the *Hello Web App* main book) but, in terms of database design, it's much better to create separate models for separate objects. If you haven't read the previous chapter, *Adding a New Model and Working With Multiple Models*, I'd recommend you do so now.

First, we need to install the package *Pillow*, which is required by Django's model field `ImageField`. (We'll learn how to use some of Pillow's functionality in the next chapter!)

Make sure you're in your virtual environment, then install Pillow with pip. This is one of the larger and more robust libraries so it's going to install a bunch of additional utilities and display a lot of text. Eventually, you should receive this as your output:

```
$ pip install Pillow
...
Downloading Pillow-2.9.0-cp27-none-macosx_10_6_intel.
macosx_10_9_intel.macosx_10_9_x86_64.macosx_1  Downloading
Pillow-2.9.0-cp27-none-macosx_10_6_intel.macosx_10_9_intel.
macosx_10_9_x86_64.macosx_10_10_intel.macosx_10_10_x86_64.whl
(2.9MB): 2.9MB downloaded
  Storing download in cache at /Users/limedaring/local/
pipcache/https%3A%2F%2Fpypi.python.org%2Fpackages%2Fcp27%2F-
P%2FPillow%2FPillow-2.9.0-cp27-none-macosx_10_6_intel.
macosx_10_9_intel.macosx_10_9_x86_64.macosx_10_10_intel.
macosx_10_10_x86_64.whl
Installing collected packages: Pillow
Successfully installed Pillow
Cleaning up...
```

Make sure to add Pillow to your *requirements.txt* too before you forget.

Now we can use `ImageField` in our models. In your *models.py*, add the following:

models.py

```python
# our helper, add above the new model
def get_image_path(instance, filename):
    return '/'.join(['thing_images', instance.thing.slug, filename])


class Upload(models.Model):
    thing = models.ForeignKey(Thing, related_name="uploads")
    image = models.ImageField(upload_to=get_image_path)
```

The model Upload has two fields, the object we're linking to in the other model, and the image itself. Note that we're not just adding the model, but also a helper function to set up the path that the file will be uploaded to. That way, we'll have a folder of images per object, rather than all the uploaded files together in one folder. Make sure to update the ForeignKey if your main model is named differently.

Tip: *Did you go through the previous chapter? Feel free to link your new Timestamp abstract model to add created and modified model fields to your Upload model!*

Migrate your database

Since you've added a new model, you need to migrate your database.

```
$ python manage.py makemigrations
Migrations for 'collection':
  0003_image.py:
    - Create model Upload
```

And then apply the migration:

```
$ python manage.py migrate
Operations to perform:
  Synchronize unmigrated apps: registration
  Apply all migrations: admin, contenttypes, collection,
```

```
  auth, sessions
Synchronizing apps without migrations:
  Creating tables...
  Installing custom SQL...
  Installing indexes...
Running migrations:
  Applying collection.0003_upload... OK
```

Showing the image in the templates

Django won't "serve" user uploaded media by default, so we need to do a few things first to make it work.

First, open your *settings.py* and add this code below your STATIC_URL variable definitions, which tells Django where to store the uploaded images:

settings.py
```
# add this if you don't have it already
BASE_DIR = os.path.dirname(os.path.dirname(os.path.abspath(__file__)))

# our new lines
MEDIA_ROOT = os.path.join(BASE_DIR, 'media')
MEDIA_URL = '/media/'
```

Next, create a "media" folder in the top level directory in your project (same area as *manage.py*) that will hold the user-uploaded media files:

```
$ mkdir media
```

Finally, we need to add a bit to our *urls.py* file to tell it to serve these user-uploaded images:

urls.py
```
# add to the top of the file
from django.conf import settings
```

```
# add to the bottom of your file
if settings.DEBUG:
    urlpatterns += [
        url(r'^media/(?P<path>.*)$', 'django.views.static.serve', {
            'document_root': settings.MEDIA_ROOT,
        }),
    ]
```

We only want to serve static files like this for development, but not in on our production/live server. You'll probably want to upload your user-uploaded files to a static files hosting solution like Amazon S3.

- If your app is deployed to Heroku, check out this resource: http://hellowebapp.com/ic/18

- Otherwise, check out Django's documentation on deploying static files: http://hellowebapp.com/ic/19

Finish this chapter first, though, before investigating how to deploy your static files!

If we load up our admin to check out the new model, it won't show up—we haven't added it to our *admin.py*. Let's do that now.

Adding the Upload model to your admin page

Add the below code to *admin.py*, which is located in the same folder as your *models.py*:

admin.py
```
# don't forget to add the model to your model imports
from collection.models import Thing, Social, Upload
```

```
# our new model to add at the bottom
class UploadAdmin(admin.ModelAdmin):
    list_display = ('thing',)
    list_display_links = ('thing',)


# and register it
admin.site.register(Upload, UploadAdmin)
```

Save the file, then check out your admin:

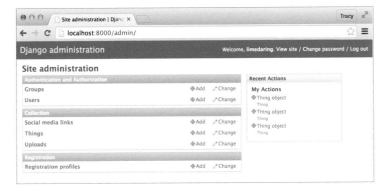

Awesome, we have a new image model! Something funny happens when we try to upload an image though:

If you went through the original *Hello Web App* tutorial, you might see something like the above screenshot. It would be much better if that dropdown showed the "name" on our Thing model. Thankfully that's an easy fix—we just need to add Django's __unicode__() method to our model

models.py
```
class Thing(models.Model):
    name = models.CharField(max_length=255)
    description = models.TextField()
    slug = models.SlugField()
    user = models.ForeignKey(User, unique=True, blank=True,
        null=True, related_name="users")


    # the new code we're adding
    def __unicode__(self):
        return self.name
```

Don't forget to add *two* underscores around "unicode." Once you save and refresh the admin, you'll see your object names instead.

Go ahead and upload an image to one of your objects in your database:

Now that we've configured everything and added the relevant settings, we can work on the template.

Setting up the template to display images

In the original *Hello Web App*, we created a view called `thing_detail` which displayed the individual object page. Update your individual object view so it grabs all the images owned by the object:

views.py

```
def thing_detail(request, slug):
    thing = Thing.objects.get(slug=slug)
    social_accounts = thing.social_accounts.all()

    # new: grab all the object's images
    uploads = thing.uploads.all()

    # and pass to the template
    return render(request, 'things/thing_detail.html', {
        'thing': thing,
        'social_accounts': social_accounts,
        'uploads': uploads, # don't forget to add me
    })
```

Let's head over to our object template (*thing_detail.html* in the original *Hello Web App* tutorial), and add in a loop that will go through all the images that we found in our database query in our view:

thing_detail.html
```
{% block content %}
<h1>{{ thing.name }}</h1>
<p>{{ thing.description }}</p>

{% comment %} our new loop {% endcomment %}
{% for upload in uploads %}
<img src="{{ upload.image.url }}" alt="" />
{% endfor %}
...
```

We're looping through every upload for this object, and for each, grabbing the "url" attribute that's on the image field in the model. Django sets this up for us automatically when we use an `ImageField`.

If you added an image when you were in the admin, open up the relevant object page on your app to check out the image:

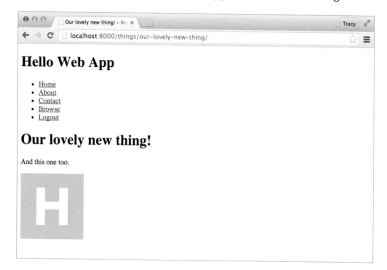

Awesome, you now have non-website static images showing up in your app! Now let's add a page to our website so users can upload files.

Uploading files in the templates

We're going to set up a page that allows us to upload new images and remove old ones, linked from our existing edit page.

Following the urls-views-template formula, let's set up a new URL first.

urls.py
```
urlpatterns = [

    . . .

    # our new url
    url(r'^things/(?P<slug>[-\w]+)/edit/images/$',
        views.edit_thing_uploads, name='edit_thing_uploads'),
```

Next, head back to our views to set up the logic for the new page. Pay attention to the comments here:

views.py
```
# add to the top
from collection.forms import ThingUploadForm
from collection.models import Upload


# add to the bottom
@login_required
def edit_thing_uploads(request, slug):
    # grab the object...
    thing = Thing.objects.get(slug=slug)

    # double checking just for security
    if thing.user != request.user:
        raise Http404
```

```
    # set the form we're using...
    form_class = ThingUploadForm

    # if we're coming to this view from a submitted form,
    if request.method == 'POST':
        # grab the data from the submitted form,
        # note the new "files" part
        form = form_class(data=request.POST,
            files=request.FILES, instance=thing)

        if form.is_valid():
            # create a new object from the submitted form
            Upload.objects.create(
                image=form.cleaned_data['image'],
                thing=thing,
            )

            return redirect('edit_thing_uploads', slug=thing.slug)

    # otherwise just create the form
    else:
        form = form_class(instance=thing)

    # grab all the object's images
    uploads = thing.uploads.all()

    # and render the template
    return render(request, 'things/edit_thing_uploads.html', {
        'thing': thing,
        'form': form,
        'uploads': uploads,
    })
```

Instead of just saving the form, we've created a new object
from the form's uploaded image. Otherwise, if we were just
displaying the form, we would display the already-upload-
ed images on the template. (This is like what we did for the

main page for this object.) This makes it easy to see what had already been uploaded.

We need to create another form for this page, so head over to *forms.py*:

forms.py
```
# make sure to import your model at the top
from collection.models import Upload


# add at the bottom
class ThingUploadForm(ModelForm):
    class Meta:
        model = Upload
        fields = ('image',)
```

We're going to use a ModelForm again, and the only field we need to display on the public-facing form is the image field—we don't need to give users the ability to change the "owner" of the form.

Finally, create a new template to hold the new form.

```
$ cd collection/templates/things
collection/templates/things $ touch edit_thing_uploads.html
```

And add the below information:

edit_thing_uploads.html
```
{% extends 'base.html' %}
{% block title %}
Edit {{ thing.name }}'s Images - {{ block.super }}
{% endblock %}

{% block content %}
<h1>Edit {{ thing.name }}'s Images</h1>
<h2>Uploaded images</h2>
```

```
{% for upload in uploads %}
<img src="{{ upload.image.url }}" alt="" />
{% endfor %}

<h2>Upload a new image</h2>
<form role="form" action="" method="post" enctype="multipart/form-data">
    {% csrf_token %}
    {{ form.as_p }}
    <input type="submit" value="Submit" />
</form>
{% endblock %}
```

Note that we're adding `enctype="multipart/form-data"` to our form which will let us upload files (our data will be properly encoded to be read by the server).

Of course, add a link to this page from your main edit page:

edit_thing.html

```
...
<a href="{% url 'edit_thing_uploads' slug=thing.slug %}">
    Edit images
</a>
```

Reload your app and you should see something like the below, after logging in as the user that owns the object with the image attached.

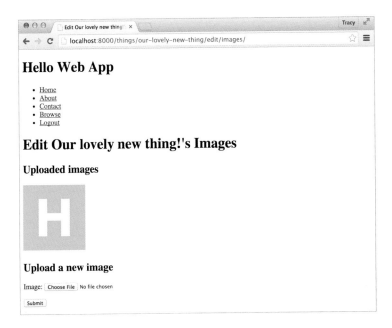

Play around with adding new images.

What if we went to delete the images we uploaded? Of course, we can do it in the admin already, but let's get the functionality built on the front-end.

We're going to add a delete link below every image shown on the edit uploads page, which'll delete that particular upload. Rather than starting with the URLs, let's add the link first since we already have the template open.

edit_thing_uploads.html

```
<h2>Uploaded images</h2>
{% for upload in uploads %}
<img src="{{ upload.image.url }}" alt="" />
<!-- our new button -->
<a href="{% url 'delete_upload' id=upload.id %}">Delete</a>
{% endfor %}
```

We're going to pass the ID of the image to a view that will delete that image and then refresh the page. Don't refresh your templates just yet because Django will throw an error because we haven't made the view yet.

Back over to *urls.py* to add the new URL:

urls.py
```
urlpatterns = [
    ...
    url(r'^things/(?P<slug>[-\w]+)/edit/images/$',
        views.edit_thing_uploads, name='edit_thing_uploads'),
    # the new url
    url(r'^delete/(?P<id>[-\w]+)/$',
        views.delete_upload, name='delete_upload'),
```

And then back over to *views.py* to add the new view:

views.py
```
@login_required
def delete_upload(request, id):
    # grab the image
    upload = Upload.objects.get(id=id)

    # security check
    if upload.thing.user != request.user:
        raise Http404

    # delete the image
    upload.delete()

    # refresh the edit page
    return redirect('edit_thing_uploads', slug=upload.thing.slug)
```

We're grabbing the Upload from the image ID, and after making sure that the owner of the Thing that the image is under is the logged in user, we'll delete the image and refresh the page.

Test it out uploading new images on the page and deleting. Unfortunately right now, users could upload a 15MB image to our app and we won't be able to do any resizing. Next chapter, we'll cover resizing and editing the photos from our app!

5 | CHAPTER 5
EDITING AND RESIZING IMAGES

WE'RE GOING TO USE THE LIBRARY PILLOW (installed in the last chapter!) to display, edit, and resize images uploaded to our app. It's kind of like Photoshop where you can check and change image formats and create thumbnails, but unfortunately without the lovely visual interface. Instead, we'll be doing everything through the command line!

Installation reminder

If you didn't go through the last chapter and haven't installed Pillow yet, make sure to do it now (and add Pillow to your *requirements.txt*):

```
$ pip install Pillow
```

From here on out, we're going to refer to Pillow as PIL. Instead of building in our app, we're going to pop into our Django shell to play around with image editing.

Testing out resizing, adding filters, and saving your images

In your top level directory (the one with *manage.py*) open up your shell, which will let us interact with Django. Note that our indicator for the command line changes from $ to >>>; it's not a part of the command you enter.

```
$ python manage.py shell
Python 2.7.8 (default, Aug 24 2014, 21:26:19)
[GCC 4.2.1 Compatible Apple LLVM 5.1 (clang-503.0.40)] on darwin
Type "help", "copyright", "credits" or "license" for more information.
(InteractiveConsole)
>>>
```

We're going to use PIL to "open" an image right in our shell, which will allow us to modify the image. First though, we need to load PIL:

```
>>> from PIL import Image
```

If nothing happens, it loaded successfully!

We need to give it the path to an image in our project. In the previous chapter, we covered adding user-uploaded images, which are stored in the */media/* folder. Take a look at the files you've uploaded to your project and find an image you wouldn't mind making updates to. Once you've found your image, load it in your shell using PIL's Image:

```
>>> original = Image.open("media/thing_images/hello/image.jpg")
```

That's the path to an image on my own computer—"hello" is the name of one of my objects.

Now that we've "loaded" the image, we can start using PIL's functions to inspect the image:

```
>>> original.format
'JPEG'
>>> original.size
(640, 626)
>>> original.mode
'RGB'
```

Using PIL we can see a bunch of the image's attributes, like whether it's a JPEG, GIF, PNG, or otherwise; the size of the image; and whether the image is using the RBG colorspace or the CMYK colorspace.

Let's play around with transforming the image. First, we're going to load ImageFilter, then we'll create a blurred version of our image using the filter:

```
>>> from PIL import ImageFilter
>>> blurred = original.filter(ImageFilter.BLUR)
```

(Note: *If you get an error, try loading a JPEG image instead—some of Pillow's filters only work on images in RGB mode. For example, PNGs are usually mode "P", or "palette." You could also look up how to convert a PNG to RGB mode with Pillow, which is certainly possible.)*

If you check out the saved images directory on your computer, this new blurred image won't show up. Run this command though, and it should pop up magically:

```
>>> blurred.show()
```

Hey look, our blurred image—very nice!

We can also rotate this image if we wished:

```
>>> blurred = blurred.rotate(45)
>>> blurred.show()
```

To save this updated image, run the following command—but make sure to give it the same path you had before so it saves in the correct directory, not the example path you see here. You can rename the file here as well. I've named the new file *blurred.jpg*.

```
>>> blurred.save("media/thing_images/hello/blurred.jpg")
```

Inspect your project and find the new image!

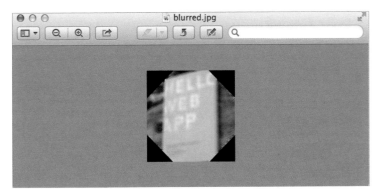

Well, it looks weird since we blurred and rotated it, but you get the idea on how to inspect, update, and save images through the shell.

Now we're going to write code to check the size of the images that our users upload, and then resize them if they're gigantic. This way, someone won't be able to upload a 40,000-pixel-width image and kill your bandwidth!

Updating your model's save method to resize images

Django has the fun ability to add extra checks and logic whenever an object is saved. We're going to write a piece of code that automatically checks uploaded images to make sure they're not too big, and resize the images if necessary.

Add this piece of code to the model holding your uploaded images:

models.py
```python
# add to the top
from PIL import Image

# our Upload model
class Upload(Timestamp):
    thing = models.ForeignKey(Thing, related_name="images")
    image = models.ImageField(upload_to=get_image_path)

    # add this bit in after our model
    def save(self, *args, **kwargs):
        # this is required when you override save functions
        super(Upload, self).save(*args, **kwargs)
        # our new code
        if self.image:
            image = Image.open(self.image)
            i_width, i_height = image.size
            max_size = (1000,1000)

            if i_width > 1000:
                image.thumbnail(max_size, Image.ANTIALIAS)
                image.save(self.image.path)
```

The `def save(self, *args, **kwargs):` and `super(Upload, self).save(*args, **kwargs)` parts are required when you override a model's save function, then you can add your new code below those bits. We first check to make sure an image exists, then check the size of the image, then we resize the image if it's too large.

Try out your app, upload a few gigantic images, and check out the size after. Magical resizing!

There are a *lot* more things you can do with the Pillow plugin, such as creating thumbnails and avatars, changing image formats, creating multiple sizes of one image, and more.

Check out some of these resources for more information on working and editing images:

- Pillow's documentation and tutorial:
  http://hellowebapp.com/ic/20

- sorl-thumbnail's documention:
  http://hellowebapp.com/ic/21

- easy-thumbnails' documentation:
  http://hellowebapp.com/ic/22

- Pillow video tutorial: http://hellowebapp.com/ic/23

Congrats on your new image editing abilities!

6 | SETTING UP DJANGO MESSAGES FOR ALERTS

ONE HANDY BUILT-IN FEATURE BY DJANGO is the messages framework. Using this allows you to set up success, error, info, etc. messages within your views to display on your templates. For example, if something didn't work, you can send over a specific error message to appear at the top of a page after a redirect.

It's fairly easy to set up, as well—this will be a short (yet sweet) chapter.

Add the messages block to your base template

We want our messages to show up on any page of our website, which means you'll be putting the template block into your *base.html*, your layout template. I'm going to put the block below right under my nav:

base.html
```
        </ul>
    </nav>
</header>

{% if messages %}
<ul class="messages">
    {% for message in messages %}
    <li{% if message.tags %}
        class="{{ message.tags }}"{% endif %}>{{ message }}</li>
    {% endfor %}
</ul>
{% endif %}
```

Basically, if Django has any messages to pass along, we're going to display them in an HTML list. The messages will come with "tags" like "error" and "info" that will allow you to mark up the message block with CSS (e.g. make it red for errors, blue for info messages, etc.)

Sending over messages from the view

We're going to update the edit view for our object (edit_thing, which we created in the original *Hello Web App* tutorial). The example should be pretty easy to follow for any view.

views.py
```
# add to the top of the page
from django.contrib import messages

# the view we're editing
@login_required
def edit_thing(request, slug):
    # grab the object...
    thing = Thing.objects.get(slug=slug)
```

```
if thing.user != request.user:
    raise Http404

# set the form we're using...
form_class = ThingForm

# if we're coming to this view from a submitted form,
if request.method == 'POST':
    # grab the data from the submitted form
    form = form_class(data=request.POST, instance=thing)

    if form.is_valid():
        # save the new data
        form.save()

        # our new message!
        messages.success(request, 'Thing details updated.')
        return redirect('thing_detail', slug=thing.slug)

# otherwise just create the form
else:
    form = form_class(instance=thing)

# and render the template
return render(request, 'things/edit_thing.html', {
    'thing': thing,
    'form': form,
})
```

Right above the redirect, we just added one line (not to mention the import statement at the top). That's it! Open up your app, log in as the user of an object, and test it out. You should get a message at the top of the page once the successful edit goes through. If you look at the source of the page, the HTML will look like this:

```
<ul class="messages">
    <li class="success">
        Thing details updated.
    </li>
</ul>
```

You can use CSS to style the message however you like.

Other message types

There are a bunch of different kinds of message formats you can use. For example:

```
messages.debug(request, '%s SQL statements were executed.' % count)
messages.info(request, 'Three credits remain in your account.')
messages.success(request, 'Profile details updated.')
messages.warning(request, 'Your account expires in three days.')
messages.error(request, 'Document deleted.')
```

And you can pass along a message whenever something happens in your view. I use this feature *everywhere* in my apps—to display all my error, success, and info messages for the user. Extremely handy!

For more about Django messages, here's the entire documentation page: http://hellowebapp.com/ic/24

7 |
FRONT-END FUN: ADDING GULP, SASS, AND BOOTSTRAP

SO FAR IN HELLO WEB APP, I've explicitly avoided doing anything with the front-end (the HTML, CSS, and JavaScript parts of a website) other than helping you add static files in the original tutorial. We've been focusing on building an app.

If you're already used to doing front-end development, you probably know that we don't just use plain ol' CSS anymore. There are a whole bunch of front-end tools like CSS preprocessors (Sass, LESS), CSS postprocessors (PostCSS, Pleeease), build systems (Gulp, Grunt), JavaScript frameworks (AngularJS, Backbone, Ember.js, React), not to mention JavaScript runtime environments that you usually use with all of the above (Node.js).

Phew.

You might have heard of the Bootstrap front-end framework, which provides a ton of utilities to websites, like a responsive-design framework (so your website can look smashing on large monitors and tiny phone screens), designed widgets, and more.

And if you're coming to Django with front-end experience, you might have been wondering this whole time how to add the tools you already know and use into your app—like Sass and Gulp—and how to make everything play nicely with each other. If so, this is the chapter for you.

We're going to set up Sass and Bootstrap, as well as the tools Bootstrap requires like Node.js and PostCSS, and in the process, we'll install the Gulp build system. If you want to install any other tools beyond what we're installing, this section will give you good hints on how to do that as well.

Quick note to those who are completely new to front-end development: I highly encourage you to work with basic HTML and CSS first before jumping into Sass and other complicated front-end systems. Sass is basically advanced CSS, and it will be a lot easier to understand CSS if you first work with it in its pure version. You might want to skip this chapter altogether and come back after you've worked with CSS for awhile. Codecademy has a great tutorial: http://hellowebapp.com/ic/25

More about the tools we're installing

Sass (http://hellowebapp.com/ic/26) calls itself a CSS extension language—it's pretty much CSS on steroids. It adds every feature you might want in CSS: nesting, variables, mixins, and more (all the things we're using in programming!) If you're not familiar with Sass yet, take a look at the Sass basics page linked above.

Bootstrap (http://hellowebapp.com/ic/27) is a front-end framework. It adds a basic, customizable design, a grid, responsiveness (which allows your website to work as seamlessly on a desktop computer as it does on a mobile phone), lots of reusable HTML components (like navbars, pagination, and progress bars), and lots of other design and layout features. Bootstrap jump-starts the design and markup of any website. If you don't know much about design, you can use the Bootstrap defaults and get a very decent (though generic) looking app—certainly leaps and bounds better than than you would get using straight HTML.

If you have some background in design, you can use Bootstrap as a framework and add a layer of customization on top of the the default Bootstrap styles. This way, your app looks unique and you save time by not building everything from scratch (this is what I do for my own projects!)

Bootstrap thankfully uses Sass, so the two tools play nicely with each other.

Additional front-end tools we'll be installing

A lot of the front-end development tools we mentioned above are not built in Python, but rather in Ruby or Node.js (which is JavaScript). Unfortunately, similar pure-Python projects are not up to par with Node.js at the moment. The web front-end community is largely independent of any particular web framework like Django, so we'll have to dive into some of the tooling they settled on.

Sass was originally Ruby project, but these days the community is migrating to a "port" of Sass, written in the C programming language, named Libsass. Libsass is much faster than the original Ruby Sass. We'll get into installation of Libsass in a second.

Bootstrap's particular usage of Sass relies on some Node.js components, and the vast majority of the front-end tools I mentioned above are also built using Node.js. We're going to avoid installing Ruby by using Libsass rather than Sass, but we're still going to need Node.js. I suspect you'll want to add other Node.js components we're not referencing here, so it will be good to get you set up with Node.js now.

Additionally, Bootstrap requires a few other utilities. The full stack we're going to install is:

1. Autoprefixer (http://hellowebapp.com/ic/28), which reads your CSS and adds browser-specific prefixes to make sure it works on all browsers. Sometimes browsers have their own CSS names—for example, if in your CSS you wanted `display: flex`, normally, you'd have to type out `display: -webkit-box; display: -webkit-flex; display: -ms-flexbox;` as well. Autoprefixer does this for you, using...

2. PostCSS (http://hellowebapp.com/ic/29). Autoprefixer is a PostCSS plugin, so you'll need to install this first, and you'll install it using...

3. Gulp (http://hellowebapp.com/ic/30), which automates front-end development tasks such as preprocessing, transpiling, minification, live-reloading, and more. And Gulp needs...

4. Node.js, mentioned before.

Phew, that is a TON of utilities. If you're asking yourself "isn't this rabbit-hole a bit excessive?" know that you're not alone. Luckily, we only need to set this up once, and we'll rarely worry about it again. Let's get started installing things, then we'll see how it all works together.

Installation

Libsass

We're going to use the libsass-python plugin (http://hellowebapp.com/ic/31) which will add Sass functionality to your project. Install it using the usual suspect:

```
$ pip install libsass
...
Successfully installed libsass
Cleaning up...
```

Node.js

You know how we use pip to install Python packages? Node.js has its own package management system called *npm*. We need to install Node.js first to access the npm package installer, which we can then use to install Gulp and other utilities.

On a Mac? Have you installed Homebrew? If you followed the *Hello Web App* original instructions for installation, you already have Homebrew. In this case, to install Node.js, type `brew install node` into your command line.

Otherwise (if you're on Mac or Linux without Homebrew, or on Windows), follow these instructions to install Node.js: http://hellowebapp.com/ic/32

Want to check whether everything is successfully installed? Run these commands:

```
$ node -v
v0.12.0
$ npm -v
2.12.1
```

You might get different version numbers depending on whether new versions came out after the printing of this book. Basically, if it doesn't give you an error message, you're good!

Just like *requirements.txt* which lists out the Python packages required by our project, we're going to create a *package.json* which lists out the npm packages we've installed. Make sure you're in your top level project directory (where *manage.py* lives), and run `npm init`. This will walk you through creating your package file. You only really need to fill out name and version (both of which should have smart defaults for you—you can just press return to accept the default values). You'll see something like this:

```
$ npm init
...
name: (hwatest3)
version: (1.0.0)
description: My app
entry point: (index.js)
test command:
git repository:
keywords:
author: Tracy Osborn
license: (ISC)
About to write to /Users/limedaring/projects/hellowebapp/
package.json:
{
  "name": "hellowebapp",
  "version": "1.0.0",
  "description": "My app",
  "main": "index.js",
  "scripts": {
    "test": "echo \"Error: no test specified\" && exit 1"
  },
  "author": "Tracy Osborn",
  "license": "ISC"
}
Is this ok? (yes)
```

Bootstrap

Now that Node.js is installed and we've created our *package.json*, let's grab Bootstrap. There is indeed an npm plugin for Bootstrap that we could install, but then that sets up our static files in a different way than we've been doing so far in *Hello Web App* (i.e. used the original *Hello Web App* tutorial, our static files are in a *static* directory within our app folder).

We're literally going to just pull the files from Bootstrap directly and insert them into our existing static directories. Head to the Bootstrap website's download page (http://hellowebapp.com/ic/33) and download the source files somewhere on your computer, like your Desktop folder—not in your project just yet.

Click on "Download source" to download the files directly from Bootstrap, somewhere on your computer—but not in your project just yet.

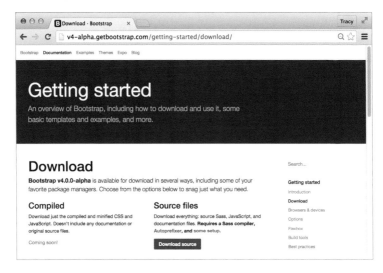

Head into your existing static directory and add a new folder to hold your your Sass (SCSS) files:

```
$ cd collection/static
collection/static $ mkdir scss
```

Then you'll need to move the files over into your project:

1. Open up your downloaded Bootstrap directory, and copy the files under */scss/* in the Bootstrap directory into your newly created */scss/* folder. You can do this in whatever way you're comfortable, through the command line or through your file system navigator like Finder on Mac or Explorer on Windows.

2. Once you're finished with this, copy the files in the */js/src/* directory into your own */js/* directory.

All other Bootstrap files can be ignored as we're going to use our own setup using Gulp, detailed below!

Gulp, PostCSS, and Autoprefixer

Instead of installing Gulp just in our project's virtualenv, we're going to install it globally (so you can use Gulp for any project moving forward):

```
$ npm install -g gulp
```

Once installed, we need to save it to our *package.json* file as a dependency for our project:

```
$ npm install --save-dev gulp
```

If you open up your *package.json*, you'll see a new section named devDependencies with Gulp listed. The command above automatically adds to this list. For example:

```
{
  "name": "hellowebapp",
  "version": "1.0.0",
  "description": "My app",
  "main": "index.js",
  "scripts": {
```

```
    "test": "echo \"Error: no test specified\" && exit 1"
  },
  "author": "Tracy Osborn",
  "license": "ISC",
  "devDependencies": {
    "gulp": "^3.9.0"
  }
}
```

Now that Gulp is installed, we can install our Gulp plugins that will add PostCSS, Autoprefixer, and other utilities we need. I split this into two commands due to the line lengths in this book, but you could do this as one command if you like.

```
$ npm install --save-dev gulp-sass gulp-concat gulp-rename
$ npm install --save-dev autoprefixer gulp-postcss
```

Now that Gulp is installed, we need to create the file that tells Gulp what to do—basically, take our Sass files and make browser-readable CSS from them. In the same top-level directory for your project (where *manage.py* lives), create `gulpfile.js`—this is the file that tells Gulp its tasks, what those tasks are, and when to run them.

```
$ touch gulpfile.js
```

I'm going to give you a basic Gulpfile, and we'll walk through the pieces of the file together.

gulpfile.js
```
// Include Gulp
var gulp = require('gulp');

// Include Our Plugins
var sass = require('gulp-sass');
var concat = require('gulp-concat');
var rename = require('gulp-rename');
```

```javascript
var autoprefixer = require('autoprefixer');
var postcss = require('gulp-postcss');
// Compile Our Sass
gulp.task('sass', function() {
    return gulp.src('collection/static/scss/*.scss')
        .pipe(sass())
        .pipe(gulp.dest('collection/static/css'));
});

// Concatenate
gulp.task('scripts', function() {
    return gulp.src('collection/static/js/*.js')
        .pipe(concat('all.js'))
        .pipe(gulp.dest('collection/static/js'));
});

// PostCSS processor
gulp.task('css', function () {
    var processors = [
        autoprefixer({browsers: ['last 1 version']}),
    ];
    return gulp.src('collection/static/css/*.css')
        .pipe(postcss(processors))
        .pipe(gulp.dest('collection/static/css'))
});

// Watch Files For Changes
gulp.task('watch', function() {
    gulp.watch('collection/static/js/*.js', ['scripts']);
    gulp.watch('collection/static/scss/*.scss', ['sass']);
    gulp.watch('collection/static/css/*.css', ['css']);
});

// Default Task
gulp.task('default', ['sass', 'css', 'scripts', 'watch']);
```

Update the paths of your static files everywhere `collection` is mentioned (`collection` being the default app in *Hello Web App* land). Change the app name and paths if necessary to match your project.

Running through the file, this is exactly what we're doing:

- First, at the top, we tell Gulp which Gulp plugins we're using. That's the `require()` blocks at the top. We then tell Gulp to use those packages and we assign the "action" to a variable that we can use in the instructions.

- Then, we set up tasks. We name the task (that's the `gulp.task('sass',` part—we're naming that task "sass"), then we create a walkthrough of the parts of that task. For example, in the `scripts` task, we tell it to grab all files in the */js/* directory, use the `gulp-concat` plugin to create one big JavaScript file named *all.js*, then save that file back in the */js/* directory.

- The Gulp task `watch` that we set up will track changes made to files and run the tasks we've set up as needed. So if we change something in our JavaScript files, Gulp will automatically run the task that combines it into our *all.js* file for us. This is why our tasks are set up in individual parts—changes to JavaScript files will trigger one set of tasks while changes to SCSS files will trigger another set of tasks.

- Finally, we tell Gulp to run these tasks that we set up when we start Gulp.

We're basically concatenating our JavaScript files into just one JS file (saving us HTTP requests that slow our site down), as well as running PostCSS and Autoprefixer on our SCSS files.

So! At this point, we've installed Sass, Node.js, Gulp, a bunch of Gulp plugins, and moved over the Bootstrap files so we can use them in our app. The last thing we need to do is copy over our pre-existing CSS file and make it a new SCSS file, so we can start working with Sass rather than CSS:

```
collection/static/scss $ cp ../css/style.css style.scss
```

To include those Bootstrap files we added before, add this import statement to the top of your *style.scss* file. This will import the *bootstrap.scss* file, which, in turn, imports the rest of the Bootstrap files.

style.scss
```
/* add to the top of the file */
@import "bootstrap";
```

Like `runserver`, we need to run Gulp for it to detect changes and update files. You just need to run this, likely in another tab of your command line, so you can run both `runserver` and `gulp` simultaneously:

```
$ gulp
[14:24:24] Using gulpfile ~/projects/hellowebapp/gulpfile.js
[14:24:24] Starting 'sass'...
[14:24:24] Starting 'css'...
[14:24:24] Starting 'scripts'...
...
```

Now you can edit the new SCSS file to your heart's content, and Gulp should detect changes to your SCSS files and compile them automatically to *style.css*, which is already linked to from your base template. Try writing some SCSS and watch the output from the Gulp task detecting those changes and writing to your *style.css* file—then you can load up your app and see the style changes applied. The last thing you need to do is link to your *all.js* file from your base template.

Your front-end development is significantly more powerful now!

Conclusion and further exploration

There isn't much in terms of screenshots to show in this chapter—a lot of it is just installing. The exploring part is up to you. If you jumped into this chapter already knowing about Bootstrap and Node.js and Gulp, you're probably good at this point. If you're still new, here are some resources:

- Bootstrap's documentation is excellent and covers everything that the framework has to offer: http://hellowebapp.com/ic/27

- There seem to be a billion-and-a-half different Node.js and Gulp plugins you can use for your development—I deliberately tried to keep this chapter simple, but if you'd like to explore more, check out npm's plugin directory (http://hellowebapp.com/ic/34) as well as Gulp's plugin directory (http://hellowebapp.com/ic/35).

- In particular, you can use gulp-livereload combined with a browser plugin to refresh your web page automatically upon changes. More info here: http://hellowebapp.com/ic/36

- New to Sass? Here's a good tutorial: http://hellowebapp.com/ic/37

You'll probably want to add the */node_modules/* folder to your *.gitignore* file — no need to track the plugins in git. Don't know what a *.gitignore* file is? Check out this resource: http://hellowebapp.com/ic/38

Enjoy your front-end improved workflow and tools!

8 READING SOURCE CODE AND SETTING UP A FORM TO EDIT USER EMAIL ADDRESSES

AT THIS POINT IN OUR WEB APP JOURNEY, we've learned how to create our own model, access it, show the information in it through templates, and create forms to update that information.

What about information outside our own model? In the original *Hello Web App* tutorial, we used Django's User model, which takes care of holding our users' email addresses, usernames, and passwords (among other things). How do we update that information?

This chapter is mainly about how we can look at the code we're importing and using on *Hello Web App* and how to figure out how to change it. We did a version of this in the original *Hello Web App*, in the chapter about registration: we *subclassed* one of the methods in the *django-registration-redux* plugin. To do this, we needed to read the original code, and we're going to do the same in this chapter.

Let's take a look at the Django code on GitHub:
http://hellowebapp.com/ic/39

/django/contrib/auth/models.py, line 366

```
class User(AbstractUser):
    """

    Users within the Django authentication system are
    represented by this model.
    Username, password and email are required. Other fields are
    optional.
    """

    class Meta(AbstractUser.Meta):
        swappable = 'AUTH_USER_MODEL'
```

That's not very helpful, but we can see that the User class is extending AbstractUser (which basically means it's an add-on to this other model). Let's take a look at AbstractUser:
http://hellowebapp.com/ic/40

/django/contrib/auth/models.py, line 297

```
class AbstractUser(AbstractBaseUser, PermissionsMixin):
    """

    An abstract base class implementing a fully featured User
    model with admin-compliant permissions.
    Username and password are required. Other fields are
    optional.
    """

    username = models.CharField(
        _('username'),
        max_length=30,
        unique=True,
        help_text=_('Required. 30 characters or fewer. Letters,
            digits and @/./+/-/_ only.'),
        validators=[
            validators.RegexValidator(
                r'^[\w.@+-]+$',
```

```
        _('Enter a valid username. This value may
        contain only ' 'letters, numbers '
        'and @/./+/-/_ characters.')
    ),
],
error_messages={
    'unique': _("A user with that username already
        exists."),
},
)
first_name = models.CharField(_('first name'),
    max_length=30, blank=True)
last_name = models.CharField(_('last name'),
    max_length=30, blank=True)
email = models.EmailField(_('email address'), blank=True)
```

That looks right—fields for username, email, first_name, and the rest of the fields that we're using within our app. I'm only showing some of the code here, but I *highly, highly* encourage you to check out the full code.

Reading other people's code is important because it will help you realize all the different ways something can be done. I'm teaching the very basic, easiest paths within *Hello Web App*, but programming in general isn't so simple. There isn't just one solution, there are *many*. While trying to read and understand all that code might sound intimidating, it's time well-spent!

You should be able to understand most of what's going on in the main Django source, though I bet you won't understand everything. That's okay—I don't understand everything, either. However, being curious will really help as you learn how to program. If you're curious about why Django's programmers did something a certain way, you can start googling or asking your friends why, and you'll often learn something new.

All right! Let's get back to setting up a form so your users can edit the email addresses they've saved on your web app.

Setting up the form

This is going to be surprisingly easy. Remember `ModelForm`s? This is all we need to do:

forms.py
```
# add to the top
from django.contrib.auth.models import User


# our new form
class EditEmailForm(ModelForm):
    class Meta:
        model = User
        fields = ('email',)
```

This is just like our other `ModelForm`s, except now we're creating a form for a model that we didn't define ourselves. We still need to import the model. Note the location of the model in GitHub: *https://github.com/django/django/blob/master/django/contrib/auth/models.py*. We're importing `User` from `django.contrib.auth.models`, and the URL is *django/contrib/auth/model*. Make sense now?

Then we tell Django we're creating a form based off of the `User` model, and we want the form to have one field: email. Feel free to add in other fields here, based on the fields listed in the `User` source code.

Setting up the view and the template

At this point you probably know what to do, so I'm going to run through this quickly. Add a new URL for the form in your *urls.py*:

urls.py
```
urlpatterns = [
    ...
    url(r'^things/(?P<slug>[-\w]+)/edit/email/$',
        views.edit_email, name='edit_email'),
```

Then, we'll create the view, which is very similar to any other view that updates a model instance.

views.py
```
# add to the top
from collection.forms import EditEmailForm

# our new view
@login_required
def edit_email(request, slug):
    user = request.user
    form_class = EditEmailForm

    if request.method == 'POST':
        form = form_class(data=request.POST, instance=user)
        if form.is_valid():
            form.save()
            messages.success(request, 'Email address updated.')
            return redirect('thing_detail', slug=slug)

    else:
        form = form_class(instance=user)

    return render(request, 'things/edit_email.html', {
        'form': form,
    })
```

Walking through the view, we:

- Grab the user who is logged in and set the form class to the new form we just made (making sure to import at the top).

- If the form is submitted, we save the submitted info, display a success message, and go back to the object that the user owns.

- Otherwise, we just display the form (filled in with the current info) and send that to the template.

Let's create that template:

```
$ cd collection/templates/things
collection/templates/things $ touch edit_email.html
```

And fill it in:

edit_email.html

```
{% extends 'base.html' %}
{% block title %}Edit email - {{ block.super }}{% endblock %}
{% block content %}
<h1>Edit email</h1>
<form role="form" action="" method="post">
    {% csrf_token %}
    {{ form.as_p }}
    <input type="submit" value="Submit" />
</form>
{% endblock %}
```

Open the page in your browser (just head straight to the URL that you set in *urls.py*, after making sure you're logged in as a user on your app).

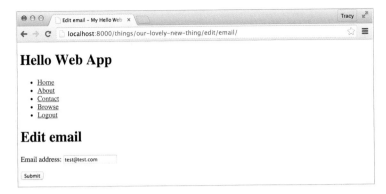

Nice! It should show the current user's email address. (Showing up blank? Make sure the user has an email address set in your admin.) You can update it and check to make sure it worked in your Django admin. We didn't add a link to this page from anywhere in the app yet, so you should do that now.

Congrats!

That was super easy, and hopefully you feel a bit more comfortable looking at Django code written by others and getting a feel for how it works. It can get a *lot* more complicated than what we've written here in *Hello Web App*. Being curious about other pieces of code and figuring out how it works is a great skill to have, so don't be afraid to look at what else exists and learn more about how to use Django!

9 ADDING PAYMENTS WITH STRIPE

One of the biggest milestones in building an app is getting your first payment from a customer. Every now and then I take a step back from the app I've built and reflect that strangers on the internet have willingly sent thousands of dollars to me in the past five years. It's such a great feeling to have revenue coming in.

If you want to take credit card payments on your app, the best way is by integrating the payment processor Stripe (http://hellowebapp.com/ic/41).

In a nutshell, this chapter is going to cover building a credit card form on our app to accept credit cards and receive a "token" in response. The token is essentially a temporary identifier for the credit card provided by Stripe. We can then use the token to charge our customers, either by recurring subscription or with one-time payments. This token allows us to charge our customers without actually seeing or storing their credit card and private details on our app—it's very important to avoid storing these details ourselves as it increases our liabilities as a business. Thanks Stripe, for taking care of that for us!

This chapter will essentially turn your app into a "freemium" business model—allowing accounts to sign up for free, and giving them the ability to "upgrade" their account by paying. This will in turn flag their account as "upgraded," which will allow you to grant extra features.

If you want everyone to pay for an account, it will be easy enough to update this tutorial to do so.

Entire books have been written about integrating Stripe and payments to web apps. This chapter is going to be the bare minimum, the fastest way for you to integrate customer payments on your app. At the end of the chapter, I'll have a list of resources that go into this topic in much more detail so you can continue building out the payments side of your business.

Quick note about HTTPS and securing your app

You might notice that, in your browser URL bar, some websites come up as `http://` and others come up as `https://`. `https://` addresses have an additional layer of security between you and the server you're connecting to—SSL encryption—meaning that interactions between you and the website are protected so that nobody else can read them even if you're using a shared WiFi at a coffeeshop.

Note: *In the context of websites, sometimes* `https://` *connections are referred to as "SSL" or "TLS" connections, but we'll refer to them as HTTPS in this guide.*

If you're using Heroku and don't have a custom domain (so your app is live as *appname.heroku.com*, you're good—you can access your app via HTTPS (so, *https://appname.heroku.com*).

However, if you're using a custom domain, and you're adding payments to your app, you need to have this extra layer of security for your users—it's one of the costs of doing business online. Unfortunately, adding that security is not easy. I'll show you the "proper" way as well as the "easy" way.

To properly add HTTPS support to your web app, you'll need to generate an SSL certificate for your site and install it on your web server:

- If you're using Heroku, they have a guide here: http://hellowebapp.com/ic/42

- If you're not using Heroku, Google for your server provider as well as "ssl certificate." You should be able to find a guide to walk you through adding SSL to your site.

As for the easy way (which is good enough for now), we can trust an outside company to do this part of security for us, like Cloudflare (http://hellowebapp.com/ic/43). Cloudflare provides, among other things, a free web performance layer on top of your app, basically caching your website and static files and making your website load faster. Cloudflare's "Universal SSL" feature lets you add HTTPS to your app without needing to buy a certificate or setting it up on your server. This is technically not as secure because we still have to trust Cloudflare to provide the guarantees they claim, but it's a very reasonable compromise for getting started.

Setting up Stripe

Once you've added HTTPS to your website, head to Stripe (http://hellowebapp.com/ic/41) and sign up for an account.

Once you've set up a username and password, you'll get a lovely Stripe dashboard:

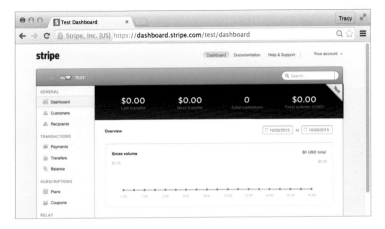

This dashboard is one of the reasons why they're the best in the industry for adding payments to your site. In one place, you'll be able to see all your paying customers, set up subscriptions, refund payments, cancel subscriptions, and more. A lot of Stripe + Django tutorials will build this functionality into your app but I personally find that the Stripe dashboard has 99% of what we need to manage the paying users on our apps.

We'll come back to the dashboard in a bit. In the meantime, let's install Stripe on our app via pip:

```
$ pip install stripe
...
Successfully installed stripe requests
Cleaning up...
```

Don't forget to add stripe to your *requirements.txt*. It's a good idea to add a specific version number—check the version that was installed by running `pip freeze`.

A note about test and live keys

Stripe will give you four keys, two pairs of "test" keys to be used in your local development, and two pairs of "live" keys to be used in production for when you deploy your app. Back in your Stripe dashboard, click on your account name in the top right, then click on "Account Settings." In your settings, there should be a tab with your API keys.

Each pair has a "secret key" and a "publishable key." The secret key must never be revealed to anybody except when speaking to the Stripe API (it's a secret between you and Stripe, like a password). The publishable key we'll be embedding in the JavaScript that our users will run.

It is very important to remember to never share or publish your secret keys. *This includes saving it in your code and pushing to a public GitHub repo.* If you accidentally published your secret keys, immediately go to the Stripe account settings and generate a fresh pair of keys. Do this even if you only leaked it for a moment, because that's all it takes. There are numerous "bots" sitting out there monitoring places like public GitHub repos so that they can steal secret keys *within milliseconds* of being published.

What can someone do with your secret keys? A malicious person with your live key can use your Stripe account and make changes, which is very, *very* bad as we're dealing with money and the accounts of our customers.

The internet can be a scary place sometimes, but we'll be just fine if we practice good habits.

There are two ways to make sure your code can use your live key without being compromised:

1. You can add it to your settings file in your repo, and if you're backing up your app in the cloud (like on Bitbucket or GitHub), now is the time to make your repo private. That way, if you push your code to the cloud for backup, your secret keys are not public.

2. Alternatively, you can set up your app to use environment variables—this way, your keys won't ever be saved in your code. Here's an article on how to do this: http://hellowebapp.com/ic/44. You'll also need to set up your server to use environment variables as well—here's an article about how to do it in Heroku: http://hellowebapp.com/ic/45

It's simpler to put everything in settings files to start, but it's a better habit to put things into environment variables even though it's a bit more complicated in the beginning.

To keep this tutorial simple, we're going to save our keys in our settings file—again, **check to make sure you're not saving your app publicly or sharing it with others**. If you can't do that, I recommend using environment variables. If you have any trouble setting them up, use the *Hello Web App* discussion forum for help: http://discuss.hellowebapp.com

Disclaimer done! Moving on.

Add your test keys to your settings

Open up your *settings.py* and add your test keys at the bottom:

```
STRIPE_SECRET = 'YOUR TEST SECRET KEY'
STRIPE_PUBLISHABLE = 'YOUR TEST PUBLISHABLE KEY'
```

Replace the YOUR TEST ___ KEY with your specific keys from Stripe, making sure they're the test keys (not live keys). Don't forget the ' characters.

Determining the payment flow

Before we step into major coding, let's figure out what we're building. In this tutorial, we're going to add a "premium" tier to our current users. We've set up the *Hello Web App* tutorial so we have Users and Things, with a User "owning" a Thing, linked via ForeignKey. Users have an edit page for their Thing, and there, they can click a button to opt into a paid monthly subscription. Once they've added their credit card and made the initial payment, their account will be marked as "premium." You'll be able to give extra features to Things marked as premium.

I'm going to show you how to set up the code to work with a one-time payment as well as a monthly subscription payment. If that's not what you specifically want (like if you want a yearly payment), it will be fairly easy to figure out how to figure out how to do it once you've gone through this walkthrough.

Set up your templates

We're going to use Stripe Checkout, a widget provided by Stripe which takes care of displaying and validating the credit card for us. As mentioned before, by using the Stripe API and only ever storing customer or card *tokens*, we can get away without ever storing the credit card information ourselves. (If you feel you might need to store credit card information specifically, you'll need to find a different credit card processing gateway and read up on *PCI compliance*.)

You can read a bit more about Stripe Checkout here:
http://hellowebapp.com/ic/46

It's super easy to add Stripe Checkout, which also saves us the trouble of designing the payment form. We're going to add the "upgrade to premium" button to our *edit_thing.html* page that we set up in the original *Hello Web App* tutorial—the edit page for our database objects that is also only accessible by the objects owner.

Add to the bottom of your edit object page:

edit_thing.html

```
<h2>Upgrade to a premium subscription?</h2>
<script src="https://checkout.stripe.com/checkout.js"
    class="stripe-button"
    data-key="{{ key }}"
    data-name="Your App name"
    data-description="Premium subscription ($19/month)"
    data-amount="1900"
    data-allow-remember-me="false"
    data-label="Upgrade to premium">
</script>
```

The above code is pretty much copy/pasted from the Stripe Checkout documentation (http://hellowebapp.com/ic/46). Basically, the fields we're using are:

- `data-key`: Your test publishable key. We'll pass this in momentarily.

- `data-name`: Replace this with your app name and the form will update.

- `data-description`: This is the description that will go at the bottom of the form.

- `data-amount`: The amount we're charging in cents. Since we're charging $19, that means the amount should be "1900."

- `data-allow-remember-me`: Stripe allows users to "save" their information among apps. Personally I find this annoying (as I don't want my users to think the information is saved by my app rather than Stripe) so I've set this to `false`.

- `data-label`: This will be your button text.

Refresh your page and a fancy button should have appeared:

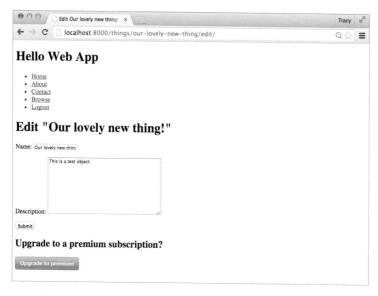

Click it, and oooh—what a fancy form:

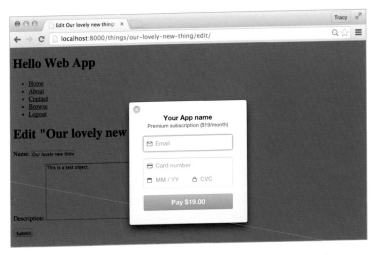

Want to test the form? When you're using a test API key, real credit cards won't work. You can use one of Stripe's test credit card numbers (such 4242 4242 4242 4242) and any other info for the rest of the fields. More test credit card numbers can be found here: http://hellowebapp.com/ic/47

The test won't work through — Stripe will whine because we never passed in our test key. Head back to your view powering the edit page, and update it to grab the test key from your *settings.py* (if you're not using environment variables) and pass it into the template:

views.py

```
# add to the top of the page in the imports
from django.conf import settings


# add to the edit object view:
def edit_thing(request, slug):

    ...
    return render(request, 'things/edit_thing.html', {
        'thing': thing,
        'form': form,
```

```
# our publishable key!
'key': settings.STRIPE_PUBLISHABLE,
})
```

Now, you can use the fake test credit card (4242 4242 4242 4242) in the form and it "works!" I wrote that in quotations because it doesn't actually do anything. The Stripe dashboard will have recorded no test payments.

Something is happening though—if you click on "Logs" in the left sidebar, you can see tokens are being created. Stripe takes the customer's credit card info, creates a unique token, then passes it back to us. We'll need to create a view that uses that token to create a charge. That might sound hard but it's pretty darn easy.

Let's wrap our payment button in a form, then we can create a view to take care of charging our customers. Don't forget to add {% csrf_token %} as well since Django requires it for security reasons on all forms.

edit_thing.html

```
<h2>Upgrade to a premium subscription?</h2>
<form action="{% url 'charge' %}" method="POST">
    {% csrf_token %}
    <script src="https://checkout.stripe.com/checkout.js"
        class="stripe-button"
        data-key="{{ key }}"
        data-name="Your App name"
        data-description="Premium subscription ($19/month)"
        data-amount="1900"
        data-allow-remember-me="false"
        data-label="Subscribe">
    </script>
</form>
```

Same Stripe script as before, now wrapped in a form pointing to the charge view. Let's create that now.

Create the URL and the view

Add your new charge URL to *urls.py*:

urls.py
```
urlpatterns = [

    ...
    url(r'^charge/$', views.charge, name='charge'),
```

Next, our logic. We're going to start easy by setting up a one-time $5 charge just so you can see how it's done, then we'll change it to match our template and change it to a recurring monthly subscription of $19/month.

First, a one-time charge:

views.py
```
# add to the top
import stripe
stripe.api_key = settings.STRIPE_SECRET

# our new view
@login_required
def charge(request):
    # grab the logged in user, and the object the user "owns"
    user = request.user
    thing = Thing.objects.get(user=user)

    if request.method != "POST":
        # we only want to handle POST requests here, go back
        return redirect('edit_thing', slug=thing.slug)
```

```python
# check to make sure we have the proper response
# from Stripe
if not 'stripeToken' in request.POST:
    # the response from Stripe doesn't have a token, abort
    messages.error(request, 'Something went wrong!')
    return redirect('edit_thing', slug=thing.slug)

# if we're cool, create a Stripe customer
customer = stripe.Customer.create(
    email=request.POST['stripeEmail'],
    source=request.POST['stripeToken'],
)

# set the amount to charge, in cents
amount = 500

# charge the customer!
charge = stripe.Charge.create(
    customer=customer.id,
    amount=amount,
    currency='usd',
    description='My one-time charge',
)

messages.success(request, 'Upgraded your account!')
return redirect('edit_thing', slug=thing.slug)
```

This view isn't powering a template, so we're not going to render anything, only redirect back to the edit page with an appropriate error message. Essentially, the view is:

- Grabbing the logged in user, then grabbing the object in the database that the user "owns."

- Checking to make sure we're submitting a form (if it's not a POST request, then we just redirect back to the edit page).

- Making sure we're getting a token in the form submission, which is the response from Stripe after we've submitted the user's credit card details.

- Creating a "customer" in Stripe, using that token.

- Setting up an amount to charge (in cents, so "500" is $5.00).

- Charging the customer, which is the object we got back from Stripe after creating the customer.

- Upon successful charge, setting a success message and redirecting back to the edit page.

Open up your template and try out the form again with your fake credit card number (4242 4242 4242 4242) and any other data for the rest of the fields.

Upon success, you can open up your Stripe dashboard and check out the "Customers" link in the left sidebar to see the new customer created, as well as the successful $5 payment. Poke around here for a bit since it's all a test environment (you can't break anything or affect real money). You can refund payments (whole or partial), add coupons to accounts with subscriptions, delete the customer, and more, all through the dashboard. It's a bit like the Django admin—a super powerful interface for your payment and paying customer information.

If we just wanted to set up one-time payments, we'd be golden, but we want to set up a monthly subscription plan. Let's do that now.

Add a plan to Stripe

You could add extra code to do this using the Stripe API, but I find it much easier to do this through the Stripe dashboard. Click on "Plans" in the left sidebar and add a subscription plan.

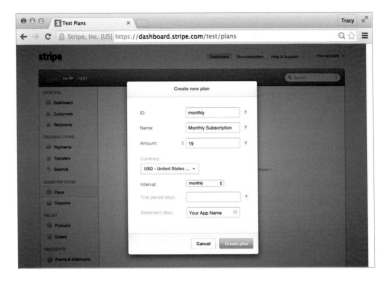

The "ID" of the plan is how we're going to reference the plan from our code.

Update your view to subscribe the customer to a plan

We're going to update our code to add a plan (the one we set up above) to our customer that we're creating. I'm going to comment out the code to charge the customer since we don't need it any more.

views.py

```
@login_required
def charge(request):
    # grab the logged in user, and the object the user "owns"
    user = request.user
    thing = Thing.objects.get(user=user)

    if request.method != "POST":
        # we only want to handle POST requests here, go back
        return redirect('edit_thing', slug=thing.slug)
```

```python
# check to make sure we have the proper response
# from Stripe
if not 'stripeToken' in request.POST:
    # the response from Stripe doesn't have a token, abort
    messages.error(request, 'Something went wrong!')
    return redirect('edit_thing', slug=thing.slug)

# create a Stripe customer and add them to a plan
customer = stripe.Customer.create(
    email=request.POST['stripeEmail'],
    source=request.POST['stripeToken'],
    # our new plan!
    plan="monthly",
)

""" our commented out code from before, no longer needed
amount = 500
charge = stripe.Charge.create(
    customer=customer.id,
    amount=amount,
    currency='usd',
    description='My one-time charge',
)
"""

messages.success(request, 'Upgraded your account!')
return redirect('edit_thing', slug=thing.slug)
```

Run another test payment on your website, then check out your Stripe dashboard. You don't need to charge the customer their first payment. If you have a subscription that charges $19/month and you create a customer and assign them to that subscription, Stripe will go ahead and charge them for you (and will continue charging every month). Super easy!

Unfortunately, as written, our code is fragile. What happens if you try to subscribe the customer to a plan that doesn't exist? It will give you an error message and throw up a 500 server error page. Let's strengthen our code in case bugs happen.

Setting up error catching

In Python, if we think an error is going to happen, we can "catch" the error to handle it and maybe display a nice error message. We're going to wrap the code where we create a customer in one of these blocks, and then send an admin email to alert us that something went wrong (using the same mail_ admins method set up in Chapter 3, *Adding Easy Admin Emails, Helpers, Sitemaps, and More*).

views.py

```
# add to the top
from django.core.mail import mail_admins

# our updated customer creation code
def charge(request):
    ...
    try:
        # create a Stripe customer
        customer = stripe.Customer.create(
            email=request.POST['stripeEmail'],
            source=request.POST['stripeToken'],
            # the monthly plan was changed to something that
            # doesn't exist
            plan="doesnotexist", # change this back to "monthly" later
        )
    except stripe.StripeError as e:
        msg = "Stripe payment error: %s" % e
        messages.error(request, msg)
        mail_admins("Error on App", msg)
        return redirect('edit_thing', slug=thing.slug)
```

Here, we're telling the code to "try" to create a customer.

- If it's successful, we're cool.

- If it isn't, then show the error to the user and send an email to the admins with the error, then refresh the page. This way the app gives meaningful feedback to the customer, rather than going to a 500 error page.

Quick side-note about Python string formatting: When we write `msg = "Stripe payment error: %s" % e`, the `%s` in the message is a string placeholder. We pass in the exception `e` as the value for the placeholder by doing `... %s" % e`. You can also do multiple placeholders like `"%s %s" % (a, b)`

We're doing the bare minimum here in terms of catching errors. We could catch the more specific errors that Stripe is passing to us and display more accurate error messages. I encourage you to read the Stripe API docs on errors here to improve your app: http://hellowebapp.com/ic/48

Add a flag to your model to indicate "upgraded" objects

At this point, a person could subscribe to the same payment plan with us over and over many times since the button doesn't disappear from their `edit` page. We really should mark the object as a paying object or "upgraded" so we can hide the credit card form, not to mention give that paying user extra features. We're going to add a flag to the model, which we'll set to `True` or `False` depending on whether this object is on a paying plan, as well as saving the ID of the customer created in Stripe.

All we need to do is add these fields to our object (`Thing` in *Hello Web App* land) in *models.py*:

models.py

```
class Thing(Timestamp):

    ...

    upgraded = models.BooleanField(default=False)

    stripe_id = models.CharField(max_length=255, blank=True)
```

Since we've changed the model, we need to create a migration and migrate our database. Django is going to ask you to populate existing rows (like we did in Chapter 3, *Adding Easy Admin Emails, Helpers, Sitemaps, and More*). Go ahead and choose option 1 to provide a default value, and then add ' ' as the default value:

```
$ python manage.py makemigrations
You are trying to add a non-nullable field 'stripe_id' to thing
without a default; we can't do that (the database needs some-
thing to populate existing rows).
Please select a fix:
 1) Provide a one-off default now (will be set on all existing
rows)
 2) Quit, and let me add a default in models.py
Select an option: 1
Please enter the default value now, as valid Python
The datetime and django.utils.timezone modules are available,
so you can do e.g. timezone.now()
>>> ''
Migrations for 'collection':
  0007_auto_20151004_0228.py:
    - Add field stripe_id to thing
    - Add field upgraded to thing
```

Then apply the migration

```
$ python manage.py migrate
Operations to perform:
  Synchronize unmigrated apps: registration
  Apply all migrations: admin, contenttypes,
```

```
  collection, auth, sessions
Synchronizing apps without migrations:
  Creating tables...
  Installing custom SQL...
  Installing indexes...
Running migrations:
  Applying collection.0007_auto_20151004_0228... OK
```

Great, now all objects in our database have a new field
"upgraded" which is set to False by default, and an empty
field to hold a Stripe ID. Let's set that to True for any account
that becomes a paying subscriber. We just need to add this to
our *views.py*:

views.py

```
# create a Stripe customer
try: customer = stripe.Customer.create(
    email=request.POST['stripeEmail'],
    source=request.POST['stripeToken'],
    plan="monthly",
)
except stripe.StripeError as e:
    msg = "Stripe payment error: %s" % e
    messages.error(request, msg)
    mail_admins("Error on App", msg)
    return redirect('edit_thing', slug=thing.slug)

# set the "upgraded" field to True and save the ID
thing.upgraded = True
thing.stripe_id = customer.id
thing.save()
```

Head to your Django admin and check out the object after
"subscribing" to a plan, and they should be marked as upgraded. Now we can hide the form on our template after successful
subscription by wrapping it in an if-statement:

edit_thing.html

```
{% if not thing.upgraded %}
<h2>Upgrade to a premium subscription?</h2>
<form action="{% url 'charge' %}" method="POST">
    {% csrf_token %}
    <script src="https://checkout.stripe.com/checkout.js"
        class="stripe-button"
        data-key="{{ key }}"
        data-name="Your App name"
        data-description="Premium subscription ($19/month)"
        data-amount="1900"
        data-allow-remember-me="false"
        data-label="Subscribe">
    </script>
</form>
{% else %}
<p>Thanks for being an upgraded member of our app!</p>
{% endif %}
```

Check it out in action:

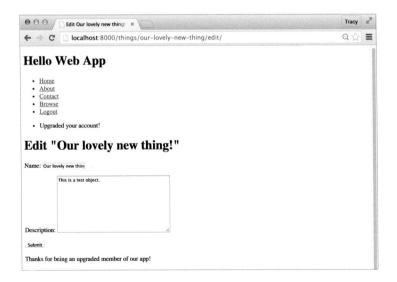

All the additional ways to improve the payment functionality on your app

You're finished with the basics! However, there is more that you could (and probably should) build into your app that we don't have room to fit into this book, such as the following:

Send a receipt upon successful payments to your customers.

Stripe can actually do this for you easily:
http://hellowebapp.com/ic/49

You can also do this yourself by using webhooks, which are described below.

Set up webhooks

Stripe, through their API, will send out "events" via webhooks to notify you when charges fail, charges succeed, and more. It's up to you to set up something to grab those notifications and I highly recommend you do so. Two common ways:

*   Set up a URL on your app for Stripe to send those notifications to. In your views, you'll need to grab the posted information, parse it, and do something with the information (for example, if a `charge.failed` notification was sent, you could email the customer automatically in your app and let them know that they need to update their credit card on file).

*   A bit easier, but not as powerful: You can use Zapier (http://hellowebapp.com/ic/50) to intercept the webhook that Stripe sends out, and email you what the webhook says. Zapier is free for a certain number of events per month (the number of times it has to do something)—this is a good alternative until you have time to build in the automatic webhook handling mentioned above.

Check out Stripe's documentation here on webhooks: http://hellowebapp.com/ic/51

Add a form for the customer to update their credit card

Often, charges will start failing if a customer changes or cancels their credit card. You'll probably want a page on your app for the customer to submit a new credit card, which will replace the old one that's on their account in Stripe. You can use the same Stripe Checkout form (updating the headline and info fields), and in your views, use Stripe to retrieve the customer using their ID you saved in the model (http://hellowebapp.com/ic/52) and then update their information (http://hellowebapp.com/ic/53).

A cancel/unsubscribe flow

Add a button for your customers to press when they want to cancel their account, which will cancel the account on Stripe's side, toggle that flag on their account on your side, and clear the `stripe_id` field on the object. Some hints on how to do this on Stripe can be found here: http://hellowebapp.com/ic/54

Additional resources and information

Phew, this was our longest chapter yet in the history of *Hello Web App*, and we didn't even cover everything. Payments are complex, but it's incredibly rewarding when you can create a web app and people start paying you.

Some additional resources to check out and continue learning:

- Stripe's examples page, with links to a lot of tutorials: http://hellowebapp.com/ic/55

- dj-stripe, a very comprehensive and powerful plugin for Django for Stripe integration: http://hellowebapp.com/ic/56

- GoDjango's video tutorial on Stripe.js: http://hellowebapp.com/ic/57

Congrats, you've added payments to your app!

As always, make sure you've committed your work. (And again, **never push your private keys to a public GitHub or similar cloud repository!** Remember my notes about environment variables and whatnot from the beginning of the chapter.)

10 | CHAPTER 10
ADDING AN API

WANT YOUR WEBSITE INFORMATION TO BE AVAILABLE to outside sources? An API is what you need! One of the reasons why Twitter got so popular was their open API when they first launched, which allowed outside developers to take their data and build new platforms upon it. For example, the original iPhone Twitter app was built by an outside developer. (Sadly they don't have an open API any more.)

Thankfully, Django (and open-source Django projects) make it easy for you to add an API to your app. This chapter will walk you through adding a very basic API that will allow outside sources to access your data, and at the end I'll point you in the direction of resources to help you continue to build out your API (e.g. if you want to allow outside sources to modify rather than just view data).

If you're not interested in building an API for your website, what we do here is easily removed so it might be worth running through this tutorial for the sake of learning.

Let's get started!

The essence of an API

I'll get into the beefy Django frameworks for building an API in a second, but first, I want to show you how easy it is to create an "API."

Essentially, an API endpoint (the URL that other services can ping to get data) simply returns data in a JSON or XML format.

All you need to do to provide data via JSON is something like this in your views:

```
from django.http import JsonResponse

def dataview(request):
    data = {'thing': 'I am a hard-coded thing.'}
    return JsonResponse(data)
```

Want to provide data from your database? You'll need to serialize it first (basically, we're translating the data into JSON format):

```
from django.core import serializers
from django.http import JsonResponse

def dataview(request, id):
    thing = Thing.objects.get(pk=id)
    data = serializers.serialize('json', [thing])
    return JsonResponse(data, safe=False)
```

You just need to point people to these URLs to have the data returned in a format where other services can read and use the JSON. This is the essence of an API, so if all you need to do is have a page with your objects in JSON format (and no need for extra API utilities like editing, creating, and deleting objects), then you might want to avoid a framework and just build it from scratch.

You'll notice that this is starting to look very similar to our normal views, except we return JSON instead of a regular HTML template. We can pass in arguments as request parameters, like what object we want to query or how many results to limit to. We can even check permissions the same way as our normal views, to make sure our user is signed in and should have access to these objects.

A simple API is great for our own website to consume, but if we want outside people to access our API, it's going to take a bit more work to build ourselves. We'll need to handle API keys, error handling, throttling, or maybe most dreadful of all—creating similar handling logic for many kinds of similar objects. What if we're fetching a User? Fetching a Thing? Fetching a Potato? Same idea as far as our API is concerned.

Luckily, there are frameworks that help us skip building these kinds of common operations by wrapping our models with "resources" that the API responds to. You'll see what I mean in a second.

Installing Django REST Framework

For a full-fledged API that allows for creating, editing, and deleting objects, we're going to use an excellent Django plugin called *Django REST Framework* (http://hellowebapp.com/ic/58) to add API functionality to our web app.

FYI, an acronym that is used here is CRUD, which stands for Create, Read, Update, and Delete—and these actions correspond with the HTTP verbs: GET (read), POST (create), PUT (update), and DELETE (delete). As you continue your journey learning about APIs, this is an important point to know!

We're going to install Django REST Framework (as usual) via pip:

```
$ pip install djangorestframework
Downloading/unpacking djangorestframework
    Downloading djangorestframework-3.2.4-py2.py3-none-any.whl
(542kB): 542kB downloaded
    Storing download in cache at /Users/limedaring/local/
pipcache/https%3A%2F%2Fpypi.python.org%2Fpackages%2Fpy2.
py3%2Fd%2Fdjangorestframework%2Fdjangorestframework-3.2.4-py2.
py3-none-any.whl
Installing collected packages: djangorestframework
Successfully installed djangorestframework
Cleaning up...
```

Once that finishes installing, we need to add it to our
INSTALLED_APPS in *settings.py*:

settings.py
```
INSTALLED_APPS = (
    ...
    'rest_framework',
)
```

Don't forget to add `rest_framework` to your *requirements.txt*.

We also need to add our API permissions to our settings. We
have the option to set our API to be accessed by anyone, by only
admins, by only those with usernames/passwords, and more.
More info: http://hellowebapp.com/ic/59

settings.py
```
REST_FRAMEWORK = {
    # Use Django's standard 'django.contrib.auth' permissions,
    # or allow read-only access for unauthenticated users.
    'DEFAULT_PERMISSION_CLASSES': [
        # we're going to use this because we're just showing data
        'rest_framework.permissions.AllowAny',
        # BUT use this one or another restricted permission if you
        # update your API to allow update and deleting
```

```
    # 'rest_framework.permissions.IsAuthenticated',
    ],
}
```

Setting up a very simple API

We're going to create a very simple API that will just show
off the objects in your database. By using Django REST
Framework, you'll have the ability to expand your API easily
if needed.

Let's add a couple basic URLs:

urls.py
```
urlpatterns = [
    ...

    url(r'^api/things/$', views.api_thing_list,
        name="api_thing_list"),
    url(r'^api/things/(?P<id>[0-9]+)/$',
        views.api_thing_detail, name="api_thing_detail"),
```

The first pattern we're going to set up will return all the objects
in our database, and the second pattern will just return the
details of one object (using its ID).

Next, we're going to set up our serializers file, which (as mentioned before), changes the data into a format that can be read
by APIs. We're going to use the default JSON format.

Add a *serializers.py* file to your app:

```
$ cd collection
collection $ touch serializers.py
```

In this file, we'll add the following:

serializers.py

```
from rest_framework import serializers
from collection.models import Thing


class ThingSerializer(serializers.HyperlinkedModelSerializer):
    class Meta:
        model = Thing
        fields = ('name', 'description', 'slug',)
```

This looks pretty close to how a `ModelForm` looks! Same idea—tie in the correct model and define which fields can be accessed.

The model and fields are taken from the model we created in the original *Hello Web App*, so update these to match your own model if needed.

Last, we need to create the views we need.

views.py

```
# add to the top
from rest_framework import status
from rest_framework.decorators import api_view
from rest_framework.response import Response


# add your new view
@api_view(['GET'])
def api_thing_list(request):
    """
    List all things
    """
    if request.method == 'GET':
        things = Thing.objects.all()
        serializer = ThingSerializer(things, many=True)
        return Response(serializer.data)
```

```
@api_view(['GET'])
def api_thing_detail(request, id):
    """
    Get a specific thing
    """
    try:
        thing = Thing.objects.get(id=id)
    except Thing.DoesNotExist:
        return Response(status=status.HTTP_404_NOT_FOUND)

    if request.method == 'GET':
        serializer = ThingSerializer(thing)
        return Response(serializer.data)
```

Here are both our views, one for displaying all objects, and one for displaying just one object. We're using a few of Django REST Framework's utilities like a decorator which allows us to specify allowed HTTP methods for security (so we can only allow GET, meaning rogue outside users can't try to DELETE our data).

In both views, we're grabbing the data that we want, passing it through the serializer that we set up to translate it to JSON, then returning the response.

Want to see your API in action? Head to *http://localhost:8000/ api/things/* (or however you named the URL) in your browser:

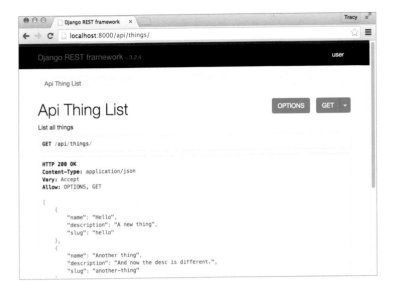

Neat, Django REST Framework made a nice looking page for us with our data! This will help the future users of our API use and navigate our API and documentation.

To interact with the API like another server would, let's play with using cURL in our command line (cURL is just a command line tool for accessing URLs).

```
$ curl http://localhost:8000/api/things/
[{"name":"Hello","description":"A new thing","slug":"hel-
lo"},{"name":"Another thing","description":"And now the
desc is different.","slug":"another-thing"},{"name":"Our
lovely new thing!","description":"And this one
too.","slug":"our-lovely-new-thing"},{"name":"spankinnew","de-
scription":"spankinnew","slug":"spankinnew"}]
```

All of our data is returned in the JSON format! You can test out your other view too:

```
$ curl http://localhost:8000/api/things/1/
{"name":"Hello","description":"A new thing","slug":"hello"}
```

Just the tip of the iceberg

What we built using Django REST Framework is *essentially* what we built just by writing our own code to return JSON at the beginning of this chapter. The advantage of Django REST Framework will come when you start building in more complicated utilities for your API, like allowing outside users to create, update, and delete objects.

To learn more about APIs and how to grow yours, check out these resources:

- Django's documentation on serialization:
  http://hellowebapp.com/ic/60

- Django's documentation on JsonResponse objects:
  http://hellowebapp.com/ic/61

- Django REST Framework: http://hellowebapp.com/ic/58

- Django REST Framework's Quickstart Guide:
  http://hellowebapp.com/ic/62

- GoDjango's post on working with JSON and Django:
  http://hellowebapp.com/ic/63

- GoDjango's video tutorial on starting an API using Django
  REST Framework: http://hellowebapp.com/ic/64

Start extending your API however you need to. As always, if you have any questions, check out our discussion forum at http://discuss.hellowebapp.com

11 | CHAPTER 11
WORKING WITH SESSIONS

SO FAR WE'VE LEARNED HOW TO BUILD THE FRONT-END of our app and tie in models, then use our views to grab information and send it to our templates to display to our users.

Sometimes, though, we need to set information and carry it between multiple pages—information that isn't stored in the database. For example, say you have a registration form that lets someone choose between a paid or a free account. Obviously, both sets of users should see a registration form. However, the customers who indicated they want to pay should also get a payment form.

How do you "save" this information across views? One option is to stick it in the database by adding a True/False field to their User model. That works, technically, but it means we'll need to access the database and we really should avoid doing that as much as possible. There's a much, much better way: save the temporary data to a session.

What are sessions?

Sessions allow you to save data to the server on a per-user basis. This isn't long term (sessions can expire), which is why we don't use it for any important data (which should go in the database). This works for both logged-in users as well as non-logged-in (anonymous) users. Once I figured out how to use sessions, I found many ways to use it for my startup to save temporary data—they're so useful.

Sessions are enabled by default in Django (thanks Django!).

Saving, accessing, and removing session data in the view

Feel free to use any view here to practice saving and accessing session data. I'm going to use our index view, since it's simple.

views.py
```python
def index(request):
    things = Thing.objects.all()
    return render(request, 'index.html', {
        'things': things,
    })
```

Saving and accessing data from the view

We're going to save an arbitrary number, then access it:

```python
def index(request):
    things = Thing.objects.all()

    # set the session
    request.session["number"] = 3

    # grabbing the session
    number = request.session["number"]
```

```
# confirming we grabbed it
print number

return render(request, 'index.html', {
    'things': things,
})
```

Refresh the homepage in your browser and take a look at your server output in your command line:

```
Starting development server at http://127.0.0.1:8000/
Quit the server with CONTROL-C.
3
[22/Aug/2015 16:53:42] "GET / HTTP/1.1" 200 1462
[22/Aug/2015 16:53:43] "GET /static/css/style.css HTTP/1.1" 200 40
```

Hey, hey, there's that 3 we set. Of course, remember that with Python, numbers don't have quotes added but strings do, so if you update it to a string, you need the " " surrounding it.

views.py
```
def index(request):
    things = Thing.objects.all()

    # set the session (this time we have quotes)
    request.session["thing"] = "This thing"

    # grabbing the session
    thing = request.session["thing"]

    # confirming we grabbed it
    print thing

    return render(request, 'index.html', {
        'things': things,
    })
```

Then check out your `runserver` output:

```
Starting development server at http://127.0.0.1:8000/
Quit the server with CONTROL-C.
This thing
[22/Aug/2015 16:55:57] "GET / HTTP/1.1" 200 1462
```

Yay!

You don't need to access the session and grab the data that it holds from the same view—you can grab from any view down the line after the initial data gets set.

Grabbing session data that might not exist yet

If you update the above code to grab a session that doesn't exist (like changing it to `thing = request.session["nope"]`, Django will throw a `KeyError` and whine that it doesn't exist.

You can update that piece of code to `thing = request.session.get("red")` (note we added a `.get` **and** changed the square brackets to parens), which, instead of throwing an error if the session doesn't exist, will instead return `None` (so then `thing` will be set to `None` and essentially not exist.)

You can also test whether the data matches a certain value. `if thing = request.session.get("red", True)` is an if-statement checking that the session variable `red` is set to the boolean `True`.

Accessing the session data in the template

Unfortunately, Django has everything set up for you to access session data in the views but not in the template by default. Head over to your *settings.py* and add these lines:

settings.py
```
import django.conf.global_settings as D_SETTINGS

TEMPLATE_CONTEXT_PROCESSORS = D_SETTINGS.TEMPLATE_CONTEXT_PROCESSORS + (
    'django.core.context_processors.request',
)
```

We're going to import Django's default settings, and basically "rename" it as D_SETTINGS. Then, we're going to find the TEMPLATE_CONTEXT_PROCESSORS variable, and *add* (note the plus sign, rather than the equals sign) django.core.context_processors.request to the list. This means we don't have to redefine the entire default TEMPLATE_CONTEXT_PROCESSORS block, we'll just make an addition to it.

With that behind us, we can see our session data in the template! You can access the data using this piece of Django template code: {{ request.session.SESSION }}. In the example we used before, we called the session thing, which means it would be {{ request.session.thing }} in the template. No need to pass it along in the render block on the view!

Removing or changing sessions

Sometimes you might want to remove or change a session. To delete a session, just use this in your views:

```
def someview(request):
    ...
    del request.session['NAME']
    request.session.modified = True
```

(Of course, replace NAME with the name/key of your session.)

For a real life example, if you have a button linking to one form and another button linking to another form, and each button sets a session variable, someone could use the back button in their browser and get *both* session variables, which might confuse your code. In this case, when you set a session variable, you can check for the other variable first and delete it.

You can also modify a session variable by just reassigning it, like any other Python variable:

```
def someview(request):
    ...
    request.session.modified = 'New name'
```

Some caveats

Sessions are saved by the browser. So, if you're testing on one browser and switch to another, the second browser won't have your saved session data.

Another issue is that the session data sticks around. If you're testing a flow, and need to start over at the beginning, heading back to the first page of the flow won't work because the sessions from before will still be saved. You need to clear your browser cookies to start over as a "clean" user.

I mentioned this before, but again, sessions can be lost if your user clears their cookies, so they're best for temporary information that you want to save between several views.

That's your rundown! Have fun using sessions as you build your app.

CHAPTER 12

12 | **CREATING YOUR OWN SCRIPTS AND A BIT ABOUT CRON JOBS**

A LOT OF WEB APPS WILL NEED TO RUN SOMETHING in the background to perform a task automatically. For example, maybe you want an email to go out every few months reminding customers to fill out missing profile information. We could do something like this manually, but it would be much better (and less time consuming for us) to do it automatically.

For something like this, we need to create a script—a piece of code that lives on its own—and run it from our command line. When I learned how to build web apps and I created my startup, I thought I was limited to building views to run web apps. But you can use Python to create pieces of code to do things for you.

In order to fulfill the *Hello Web App* paperback book orders, I wrote a piece of code that takes a spreadsheet, creates labels, and outputs the images for me to print from my computer. Before this script was created, I laboriously filled out individual forms on the USPS website. Being able to program a script to help with these kinds of tasks has saved me a ton of time in the long run.

Let's say you write a script for your web app. This script searches all your user accounts, sees whether they've logged in recently, and sends an email encouraging them to come back if they haven't. You can run this script manually, or schedule your web app server to run the script at regular intervals on your behalf. You might have heard of the term *cron job*—Cron is the task scheduler that lives on UNIX servers, and a cron job is the task it runs.

In this chapter, I'm going to walk you through the process of creating a Django command (essentially a script using Django), which Django will run (just like runserver, we'll have python manage.py script_name), then we're going to look at how we can run this script automatically through our web servers. Let's get started!

Creating a script

To create scripts using Django (a management command), we need to stick them in a specific folder under our app. Create a *management* folder under your app, add an empty *__init__. py* (which tells Python this is a Python module), create a *commands* folder within *management*, and finally, create an *email_reminder.py* file as well as another *__init__.py* file within *commands*. Phew!

```
$ cd collection
collection $ mkdir management
collection $ cd management
collection/management $ mkdir commands
collection/management $ touch __init__.py
collection/management $ cd commands
collection/management/commands $ touch email_reminder.py
collection/management/commands $ touch __init__.py
```

This seems more complicated than it should be, but that's the way it's set up in Django!

The name of our file (*email_reminder.py*) will be the name of the command we'll run using Django—so it will be `python manage.py email_reminder`. We'll come back to this in a second.

Now let's edit our *email_reminder.py* to run the task we want.

email_reminder.py

```python
from datetime import timedelta
from django.core.mail import send_mail
from django.core.management.base import BaseCommand
from django.contrib.auth.models import User
from django.utils.timezone import now
from django.template.loader import get_template
from django.template import Context


def email_tardy_users():
    two_weeks_ago = now() - timedelta(days=14)
    tardy_users = User.objects.filter(last_login__lt=two_weeks_ago)

    print "Found " + str(len(tardy_users)) + " tardy users"

    for user in tardy_users:
        template = get_template('login_reminder.txt')
        context = Context({
            'username': user.username,
        })
        content = template.render(context)
        send_mail(
            'You have not logged in in two weeks - can we help?',
            content,
            'Your app <hi@yourapp.com>',
            [user.email],
        )
```

```
class Command(BaseCommand):
    def handle(self, *args, **options):
        print "Emailing tardy users"
        email_tardy_users()
```

Wowee, that's a lot! We're also doing quite a few things you may not have seen before. Let's walk through this:

1. Start reading at `class Command`—it's at the bottom of the file, but this is actually what Django will run first. Django will look for `class Command(BaseCommand)`, and `def handle(self, *args, **options)` for your script. Within `handle` we can write what we want to do.

2. We *could* just start adding our code under `handle`, but I decided to put it in its own function, which `handle` then calls. With larger scripts, it's handy to break out bits into their own little areas, which makes reading through the commands a lot easier.

3. Take a look at `email_tardy_users()`. We're using some Django functions (loaded at the top) to get the date two weeks ago from today. Then we're searching our `User` database for users who logged in before that date (`last_login` is provided by Django on the `User` model, and `__lt` means "less than").

4. Then, we're looping through those users and sending an email.

5. Also, I added some print statements just so we can see some output when we run the command ourselves.

Before doing anything, create the template we mentioned in the code:

```
$ cd collection/templates
collection/templates $ touch login_reminder.txt
```

login_reminder.txt

```
Hi {{ username }}!

We noticed it's been awhile since you logged in. Is there any-
thing we can help you with? Feel free to respond to this email
and let us know how we can improve!

Cheers,
-The App Team
```

Cool, we should be good to go! Head back to your command line, make sure you're in the same directory as *manage.py*, and run your new command:

```
$ python manage.py email_reminder
Emailing tardy users
Found 3 tardy users
MIME-Version: 1.0 Content-Type: text/plain; charset="utf-8"
Content-Transfer-Encoding: 7bit
...
```

Note: your output will likely be different than the above depending on the users in your database. In mine, I found three users who hadn't logged in for at least two weeks, then my app sent emails to them. Yay!

Now this was run locally, so we're working off test data. Once you push this new command to your live app server and run the command, it will run for real. If you're deployed on Heroku, you can run `heroku run python manage.py email_reminder`, and if you're on a different kind of web server, you'll probably have to log in first to run the command.

Now you know how to create new Django commands to run processes—congrats!

Setting up scheduling to run the script automatically

This part is a little more difficult to explain succinctly in one chapter. How you schedule your tasks will be determined by your host, and some hosts do it differently than others.

Heroku

If you're using Heroku (http://hellowebapp.com/ic/65) as your host, they don't use Cron—they use a custom add-on called Scheduler: http://hellowebapp.com/ic/66

Once you install this add-on, you can tell it (via the website or through the command line) to run your task (`python manage. py email_reminder`) at the interval you'd like. You can read more about this in a great blog post: http://hellowebapp.com/ic/67

Other servers that use Cron

For the rest of us that use Unix-based servers (which should be nearly everyone), we have a process called Cron, which is weirdly named but pretty cool. As mentioned before, cron jobs are tasks run on the server and Cron is the scheduler itself.

With these server setups, scheduling these tasks is a bit more difficult and takes more manual work.

First, we need to set up a configuration file called a "crontab" to hold the instructions for the cron jobs we want to run (where this file lives will depend on your server). Each line we add will tell cron how and when to run a task, and it's rather hard to understand at first. For example:

```
30 11 * * * /your/directory/whatever.pl
```

Say it with me: Whaaaaaat.

Basically, cron jobs are defined like this in one non-breaking line:

```
minute hour day month day-of-week command-line-to-execute
```

The `/your/directory/whatever.pl` is the command in this example. The rest of the numbers and asterisks are representing the date and times to run the command.

First, think of `*` as "every." Reading `30 11 * * *` then would be "30th minute, 11th hour, every day of the month, every month, every day of week"—so, this script is set to run at 11:30am every day.

What would `56 18 30 1 *` be? "56th minute on the 18th hour on the 30th day of the first month, every day of the week"—so the script is set to run on January 30th at 6:56pm (as cron uses 24-hour time).

The day of the month and the day of the week look like they contradict themselves—a task set to `56 18 30 1 3` would run on January 30th at 6:56pm **and** on every Wednesday (the third day of the week.) In general, either a specific date in a month **or** a specific date in a week are chosen, rather than both at the same time. To run something every Thursday at 3:00pm, you would set the task to `0 3 * * 4`—zeroth minute of the third hour, every day, every month, on Thursdays.

Once you figure this all out, it's kind of cool, right?

Now that we've figured out how to schedule the timing, we need to tell it to run the right command; specifically, the Django management command we set up earlier.

Now that we've gone through all this, we're actually going to (mostly) throw it away and use a Django plugin instead. You can tell Cron to run your management command, but it's more complicated than I would like, and an alternative exists. Check out *django-crontab*, which allows you to set up Cron tasks in your settings file (using the timing notification we went through above, so this section hasn't been a total waste), and point it to your management command.

I'm not going to walk you through this since the documentation is pretty good. Check it out here:
http://hellowebapp.com/ic/68

Servers that don't use Cron (i.e. Windows)

Windows uses something called *Scheduled Tasks* rather than Cron. It's even more of a pain to set up (sorry). Thankfully, it's really, really rare that you'll be running your app on a Windows server. If you happen to be doing so, check out the service *EasyCron* to add the Cron ability to your server:
http://hellowebapp.com/ic/69

A note about normal scripts, not Django management commands

Earlier in this chapter, I talked about how fun it is to create little programming scripts for myself, and a lot of these don't use Django. We went over how to create a Django management command which uses your app, but you can write your own scripts using just Python.

You can create an arbitrary file placed anywhere, like this one:

hello_world.py
```
print "hello world"
```

Then you can run this via the command line like so, which should print out your "hello world":

```
$ python hello_world.py
Hello World
```

This is how you'll start programming without being attached to Django! If you already have a lot of Python experience, you might be thinking, "Well duh," but really, moving beyond Django programming into pure Python programming took me about three years. Building web apps is just too much fun!

A great resource on learning how to use scripts to automate tasks is *Automate the Boring Stuff with Python* by Al Sweigart: http://hellowebapp.com/ic/70

Now you know how to create a custom management command that you can run with Django, as well as tips on how to set up that command to run at scheduled times on your server. Enjoy your new powers!

CHAPTER 13
DATABASE PITFALLS

SAY YOU'VE LAUNCHED YOUR APP (CONGRATS!) and people are using it (super congrats!). However, when you load a few pages, it takes *forever*. You've already checked all the usual front-end suspects and the size of your website isn't that big. What's going on?

Your database might be slowing you down. Every time you have to query for information from your database, your app gets a little slower to respond. When you have a full-fledged web app with multiple models, you might be querying several different databases on just one page.

What to do?

Getting information about your queries with the Django Debug Toolbar

There is a really great plugin called the *Django Debug Toolbar* (http://hellowebapp.com/ic/71) that will help you see your database queries (not to mention a whole bunch of other issues). You can install it via pip:

```
$ pip install django-debug-toolbar
```

Then add to your `INSTALLED_APPS` in *settings.py*, making sure it comes after `'django.contrib.staticfiles'`,:

settings.py
```
INSTALLED_APPS = (
    ...
    'django.contrib.staticfiles',
    ...
    'debug_toolbar',
)
```

No need to add `debug_toolbar` to your *requirements.txt* as we only want to run it locally. Feel free to add it to your local requirements file if you have multiple though!

Now start your local server (`python manage.py runserver`) and reload your local app:

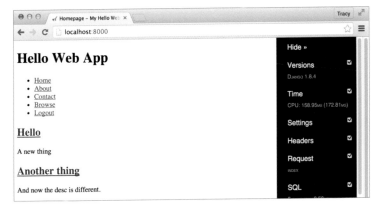

Boom, an informative toolbar! Click on some of the tabs on the right and check out all the information it gives you regarding your app. This is a useful utility to have enabled for all local development.

The main thing we're looking at right now is the number of queries we're performing on the page, which you can see under the SQL tab:

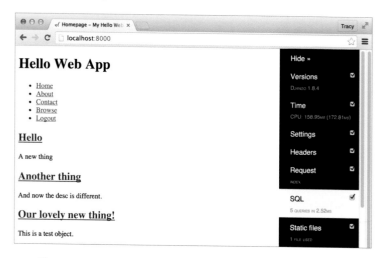

Three queries for this page isn't that bad. The problem really starts happening once you have multiple models (like what we set up in Chapter 2, *Adding a New Moodel and Working With Multiple Models*).

Optimizing queries

Right now our homepage just grabs all the objects in our database, and lists them out. Here's the view:

views.py
```
def index(request):
    things = Thing.objects.all()
    return render(request, 'index.html', {
        'things': things,
    })
```

And our HTML on our template:

index.html

```
. . .
{% for thing in things %}
    <h2><a href="{% url 'thing_detail' slug=thing.slug %}">
        {{ thing.name }}
    </a></h2>
    <p>{{ thing.description }}</p>
{% endfor %}
```

We're going to update that HTML to *also* grab all the social media accounts connected to the object and list them out too:

index.html

```
. . .
{% for thing in things %}
    <h2><a href="{% url 'thing_detail' slug=thing.slug %}">
        {{ thing.name }}
    </a></h2>
    <p>{{ thing.description }}</p>
    {% if thing.social_accounts %}
    <ul>
        {% for account in thing.social_accounts.all %}
        <li>{{ account.network|title }}</li>
        {% endfor %}
    </ul>
    {% endif %}
{% endfor %}
```

Which totally works. But wait, what happened to our database queries?

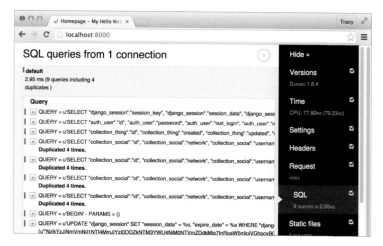

Suddenly, we're at nine database queries! Check out the information on the left (after you click on the SQL link in the right sidebar)—for *every* `Thing` we're grabbing from the database, Django is querying the `Social` database for the `Thing`'s accounts. Basically, Django is going, "Okay, grab all the things, and then for this thing, grab the social accounts, then for this thing, grab the social accounts, then for this thing, grab the social accounts..."

Once your web app has hundreds of objects, you can imagine how doing a separate query for each object when you're just rendering one template would make things *super slow*.

But we can make it better! We're going to use Django's `prefetch_related` (http://hellowebapp.com/ic/72) on our initial `Thing` query to grab everything in advance. Update your view:

views.py

```
def index(request):
    things = Thing.objects.prefetch_related(
        'social_accounts').all()
```

```
return render(request, 'index.html', {
    'things': things,
})
```

Refresh your page, and voilà—the number of queries drops.

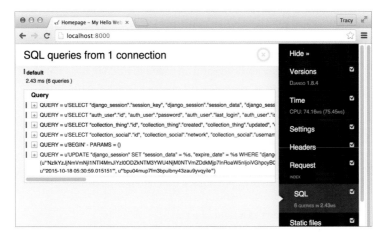

Now, Django is saying, "Okay, grab all the things, and while we're here, grab all the social accounts too." Instead of doing a query on the `Social` table every time we display a `Thing`, we've "prefetched" the results in one additional query. Now Django can just list the results out from memory.

Other optimization methods

`prefetch_related` works best here since we have what's known as a "reverse `ForeignKey`" relationship between `Thing` and `Social`. `Social` is linked to `Thing` using `ForeignKey`, but technically `Thing` is not linked to `Social`—it's a one-way arrow.

In the last example, we were listing out `Thing`s and then grabbing the social accounts. Now say we were grabbing social accounts, and then listing the `Thing`'s descriptions. As `Social` points to `Thing` (we're going in the same direction as the connection), we can use Django's `select_related` (http://hellowebapp.com/ic/73). For example: `socials = Social.objects.select_related('thing').all()`

`select_related` is better than `prefetch_related` because `prefetch_related` will do two queries (one on each database), but `select_related` will be able to do everything in *one* query since we're going along that one-way arrow.

We also have the ability to add an index to our database fields which will help our database run queries faster. An index is like a table of contents in a book—when you're looking for a specific value, you flip to the table of contents and quickly look up the page number so you can jump straight to it. Someday when there are thousands or even millions of rows in your database, a query without an index could take minutes. A proper index can bring that back down to milliseconds.

You add an index to a field like this:

```
class Thing(models.Model):
    name = models.CharField(db_index=True, max_length=255)
```

Django automatically adds an index to any model field that is a `SlugField`, or is set to `unique=True`, or is a `ForeignKey` relationship. The above is a great place to add an index, as it's not a `SlugField`, isn't set to `unique=True`, or a `ForeignKey`, and we're likely to run queries which filter by our name field.

This really is only the tip of the iceberg. Reducing queries becomes a big deal when your web app makes it big (since response and rendering time is so crucial) so there are a *ton* of ways to improve it. I highly recommend you check out Django's resource page on database optimization to see what other methods are available to improve the number of queries you make: http://hellowebapp.com/ic/74

As you work on your app, keep an eye on the number of queries your web app makes using the Django Debug Toolbar and make improvements as necessary when your queries get too large—it's one of the best things you can do for the speed of your website!

CHAPTER 14
ADDITIONAL INFORMATION AND RESOURCES

ANOTHER BOOK DOWN! CONGRATS ON GETTING THIS FAR—I'm proud of you. It's not over yet, though. You need to continue growing and improving your web app! Here's a mishmash of information and additional resources to help you in moving forward.

Different versions and updates—what should I do?

A lot of wonderful people work on both Python and Django and are making improvements all the time. These improvements get released periodically with a new version number, sometimes quite often—I'm looking at you, Django. I started writing *Hello Web App* when it was Django 1.6 and now Django 1.9 is already out.

Django updates

When Django updates, what does that mean for your app? You don't *have* to upgrade. As long as the version that works for your app is specified in your *requirements.py*, anyone who needs to install your app will know the specific Django to use for it to work.

But, these Django updates usually come with newer and better functionality, not to mention security updates that can be pretty crucial. Thankfully, Django developers are pretty savvy about making sure updates are usually backwards compatible, especially if it's a minor version update (like say, going from 1.7.1 to 1.7.2). For minor updates like these, you can almost always just install the new Django in your app (`pip install Django==VERSIONNUMBER` then update your *requirements.txt*) and everything should be peachy.

Major releases (like 1.7 to 1.8) usually come with non-backwards compatible updates. For these, the only solution is to check out the release notes (http://hellowebapp.com/ic/75) to see what was updated, especially the section on backwards incompatible changes. Then you'll just need to install the new version of Django, see what breaks, and make fixes and updates to your app. It can be a bit frustrating, especially if your previously working app suddenly stops working and you can't figure out why. There's always our *Hello Web App* discussion board if you need some help: http://discuss.hellowebapp.com

Python 3 and other updates

Hello Web App uses Python 2.7, but Python 3.4 is out. What's up with that?

The update from Python 2 to 3 was a fairly major release and a *lot* of beginner resources on the web are still using 2.7. It's still used very often, though slowly people are transitioning over to Python 3.4. *Hello Web App* uses 2.7 because the majority of the resources that you, dear reader, will be using will probably still be on Python 2.7 for at least a few more years as Python 3 usage catches on and major projects are migrated.

That said, *Hello Web App* is very nearly Python 3 compatible—one of the biggest differences between Python 2 and Python 3 is how print statements work:

```
# python 2
print "hello world"
# python 3
print("hello world")
```

So that's why we're using 2.7 for now even though a new version of Python is out. For more information about the differences, check out Python's page on the differences: http://hellowebapp.com/ic/76

Curious about Python 3? Here's a good tutorial: http://hellowebapp.com/ic/77

Other resources

Now let's move on to more awesome tutorials and Django resources!

Books

Two Scoops of Django by Audrey Roy Greenfeld and Daniel Greenfeld: http://hellowebapp.com/ic/78
I recommended this in the original *Hello Web App* and I'm recommending it again here. *Hello Web App* skirts a lot of "best practices" in favor of making things easier, and *Two Scoops* will teach you those best practices that we missed. This should be a required resource for any web app programmer using Django.

Automate the Boring Stuff with Python by Al Sweigart:
http://hellowebapp.com/ic/79
We briefly mentioned creating your own scripts in Chapter 12, *Creating Your Own Scripts and a Bit About Cron Jobs*. This book

focuses on building programs that will help you automate anything monotonous.

Effective Python: 59 Specific Ways to Write Better Python by Brett Slatkin: http://hellowebapp.com/ic/80
This book will help you move beyond just building web apps with Django to becoming a fully-fledged Python programmer. This book is great for anyone who wants to become a software engineer.

Python Cookbook by David Beazley and Brian K. Jones: http://hellowebapp.com/ic/81
Another great intermediate-level Python book to help you learn how to write Python programs and algorithms.

Online courses and tutorials

GoDjango: http://hellowebapp.com/ic/82
A great general resource with screencasts and video tutorials covering beginner to advanced Django and Python.

Learn the Command Line by Codecademy: http://hellowebapp.com/ic/83
We've gone over the basics of the command line already, but this tutorial will make you feel like a badass wizard and really increase your knowledge about what you can do through the command line.

Intro to Relational Databases by Udacity: http://hellowebapp.com/ic/84
We started delving into database design and best practices, but this tutorial will really launch your understanding about what it means to work with databases.

Treehouse: http://hellowebapp.com/ic/85
This isn't free (starts at $25/month) They cover almost every-

thing in tech—from design and front-end development to Python, Javascript, and more.

Learn Regex The Hard Way by Zed A. Shaw:

http://hellowebapp.com/ic/86
By the same author of *Learn Python the Hard Way*, this is a great way to learn about Regex (you know, that funky bit in your URLpatterns).

Learn SQL The Hard Way by Zed A. Shaw:

http://hellowebapp.com/ic/87
Also by the same author. You can use this online book to teach yourself SQL, basically the language of our databases.

Keep in touch with Hello Web App!

Check out *Hello Web App*'s website if you haven't already (http://hellowebapp.com) and sign up for the newsletter—I send announcements of workshops, new books, and free tutorials fairly regularly.

Don't forget about the *Hello Web App* discussion forums (http://discuss.hellowebapp.com). Show off your web app—I'd love to see it!

You can also keep in touch with me through the *Hello Web App* Twitter account (http://twitter.com/hellowebapp) or through my personal account (http://twitter.com/limedaring).

Best of luck building and growing your web apps, and keep in touch!

This book would not be possible without the support of many amazing people and organizations. First and foremost, thank you to the Django and Python community, a truly tremendous group of people who made this book possible.

Super thanks to Hello Web App's sponsors

I also thank these amazing organizations and companies that sponsored the new book.

Huge thanks to Opbeat (https://opbeat.com) for sponsoring this book. I got to meet a few of their team at DjangoCon US and they were some of the nicest people I've ever met.

In a nutshell, Opbeat provides application monitoring for developers. If you have a large app, Opbeat helps you track performance metrics, release tracking, and error logging, and includes an awesome looking and easy to use dashboard. It's a great service to add for anyone whose app has grown.

Django Software Foundation

Another big thanks to the Django Software Foundation (https://djangoproject.com/). The DSF (of which I am a developer member) is a non-profit organization that runs, promotes, and supports Django and projects like these.

Thanks to Hello Web App's book reviewers, editors, and testers

This book would not be as coherent and understandable if it weren't for a veritable army of reviewers, testers, and editors. The folks below muddled through my drafts with patience and understanding and helped me craft the content into something a thousand times better. Thank you to everyone below for taking the time to help me:

Andrey Petrov
Al Sweigart
Alicia Lakomski
Jody Zolli
Joel Burton
John F Croston III

Kenneth Love
Lacey Williams Henschel
Larry Ullman
Matthew Oliphant
Michael J. Metts
Michael McHugh

Last but not least, thanks to Hello Web App's Kickstarter backers

One of the biggest challenges of self-publishing a book is finding funding. Thank you to all those who donated to the second *Hello Web App* Kickstarter campaign—your donations went directly to the production of this book as well as supporting *Hello Web App* workshops worldwide.

REFERENCES

For reference, the shortened link URLs throughout the book and their related long URL are listed below.

Introduction

1 https://git-for-windows.github.io/

Chapter 1

2 https://docs.djangoproject.com/en/1.8/ref/forms/fields/
3 http://www.pydanny.com/overloading-form-fields.html
4 https://sendgrid.com/
5 https://www.mandrill.com/
6 https://sendgrid.com/docs/Integrate/Frameworks/django.html

Chapter 2

7 https://docs.djangoproject.com/en/1.8/ref/models/options/

Chapter 3

8 https://docs.djangoproject.com/en/1.8/ref/models/instances/#get-absolute-url
9 https://www.google.com/webmasters/tools/
10 http://www.sitemaps.org/
11 https://docs.djangoproject.com/en/1.8/ref/contrib/sitemaps/
12 http://lgiordani.com/blog/2013/10/28/digging-up-django-class-based-views-1/
13 https://docs.djangoproject.com/en/1.9/ref/class-based-views/generic-display/#listview
14 https://docs.djangoproject.com/en/1.9/topics/class-based-views/intro/
15 https://ccbv.co.uk/

16 https://godjango.com/15-class-based-views-part-1-templateview-
and-redirectview/

17 https://hellowebapp.com/news/tutorial-class-based-views

Chapter 4

18 https://devcenter.heroku.com/articles/s3-upload-python

19 https://docs.djangoproject.com/en/1.8/howto/static-files/deploy-
ment/

Chapter 5

20 http://pillow.readthedocs.org/en/latest/handbook/tutorial.html

21 https://github.com/mariocesar/sorl-thumbnail

22 https://github.com/SmileyChris/easy-thumbnails

23 https://www.youtube.com/watch?v=_H9uPRJWMNk

Chapter 6

24 https://docs.djangoproject.com/en/1.8/ref/contrib/messages/

Chapter 7

25 https://www.codecademy.com/tracks/web

26 http://sass-lang.com/

27 http://getbootstrap.com/

28 https://github.com/postcss/autoprefixer

29 https://github.com/postcss/postcss

30 http://gulpjs.com/

31 https://github.com/dahlia/libsass-python

32 http://howtonode.org/how-to-install-nodejs

33 http://v4-alpha.getbootstrap.com/getting-started/download/

34 https://www.npmjs.com/

35 http://gulpjs.com/plugins/

36 https://www.npmjs.com/package/gulp-livereload

37 http://sass-lang.com/guide

38 https://help.github.com/articles/ignoring-files/

Chapter 8

39 https://github.com/django/django/blob/58195f0b16999245ad-a6bd010b71c9c5352ae608/django/contrib/auth/models.py#L366

40 https://github.com/django/django/blob/58195f0b16999245ad-a6bd010b71c9c5352ae608/django/contrib/auth/models.py#L297

Chapter 9

41 https://stripe.com

42 https://devcenter.heroku.com/articles/ssl-endpoint

43 https://cloudflare.com

44 http://andrewtorkbaker.com/using-environment-vari-ables-with-django-settings

45 https://devcenter.heroku.com/articles/config-vars

46 https://stripe.com/checkout

47 https://stripe.com/docs/testing#cards

48 https://stripe.com/docs/api/python#errors

49 https://stripe.com/blog/improved-email-receipts

50 https://zapier.com/

51 https://stripe.com/docs/webhooks

52 https://stripe.com/docs/api/python#retrieve_customer

53 https://stripe.com/docs/api/python#update_customer

54 https://stripe.com/docs/guides/subscriptions#canceling-sub-scriptions

55 https://stripe.com/docs/examples

56 http://dj-stripe.readthedocs.org/

57 https://godjango.com/57-starting-with-stripejs/

Chapter 10

58 http://www.django-rest-framework.org/

59 http://www.django-rest-framework.org/api-guide/permissions/

60 https://docs.djangoproject.com/en/1.8/topics/serialization/

61 https://docs.djangoproject.com/en/1.8/ref/request-response/#-jsonresponse-objects

62 http://www.django-rest-framework.org/tutorial/quickstart/

63 https://godjango.com/blog/working-with-json-and-django/

64 https://godjango.com/41-start-your-api-django-rest-framework-part-1/

Chapter 12

65 http://heroku.com
66 https://addons.heroku.com/scheduler
67 http://guidovanoorschot.nl/adding-cron-jobs-to-a-django-project-with-heroku-scheduler/
68 https://github.com/kraiz/django-crontab
69 https://www.easycron.com/
70 http://amzn.to/1LQKpvW

Chapter 13

71 http://django-debug-toolbar.readthedocs.org/
72 https://docs.djangoproject.com/en/1.8/ref/models/query-sets/#prefetch-related
73 https://docs.djangoproject.com/en/1.8/ref/models/query-sets/#select-related
74 https://docs.djangoproject.com/en/1.8/topics/db/optimization/

Chapter 14

75 https://docs.djangoproject.com/en/stable/releases/
76 https://wiki.python.org/moin/Python2orPython3
77 http://www.diveintopython3.net/
78 http://amzn.to/1JNoNHK
79 http://amzn.to/1OgbQRr
80 http://amzn.to/1OgbXfT
81 http://amzn.to/1jIeAub
82 https://godjango.com
83 https://www.codecademy.com/courses/learn-the-command-line
84 https://www.udacity.com/course/intro-to-relational-databases–ud197
85 https://teamtreehouse.com/
86 http://regex.learncodethehardway.org/
87 http://sql.learncodethehardway.org/

INDEX